CLASS DEGREES

EVAN WATKINS

Class

DEGREES

Smart Work, Managed Choice, and the Transformation of Higher Education

FORDHAM UNIVERSITY PRESS

New York   *2008*

Copyright © 2008 Fordham University Press

All rights reserved. No part of this publication may be reproduced, stored in a retrieval system, or transmitted in any form or by any means—electronic, mechanical, photocopy, recording, or any other—except for brief quotations in printed reviews, without the prior permission of the publisher.

Library of Congress Cataloging-in-Publication Data

Watkins, Evan, 1946–
  Class degrees : smart work, managed identities, and the transformation of higher education / Evan Watkins.
      p.   cm.
  Includes bibliographical references and index.
  ISBN 978-0-8232-2982-6 (cloth : alk. paper)—ISBN 978-0-8232-2983-3 (pbk. : alk. paper)   1. Vocational guidance.   2. Occupational training.   3. Competition (Psychology)   I. Title.
LC1043.W38   2008
371.4′25—dc22
                                                                                    2008016404

Printed in the United States of America
10 09 08   5 4 3 2 1
First edition

for Diane

CONTENTS

Acknowledgments ix

1. We're Going to the Show — 1
2. New Selves / Old Selves, Class Dreams / Class Nightmares — 17
3. School to Work to School to Work to . . . — 39
4. How the Inequality Connection Was Timed Out — 60
5. Class Processes 101: The Purpose of Competition — 74
6. Competition, Choice, and the Management of Class Doubling — 92

References — 119

Index — 123

ACKNOWLEDGMENTS

Among so many colleagues and friends who have contributed so much, I want especially to thank Marco Abel, Amitava Kumar, John Muckelbauer, and Jeff Nealon, who put up with hearing me go on and on about all kinds of vague ideas and somehow managed to sort out and identify what might work together for a book. I first began thinking about these ideas in conversations with Jan Radway. David Ruccio, as usual, gave me a great deal of support and shared generously his considerable expertise. Gregory McNamee has been a superb reader, and I am greatly pleased to be working with Helen Tartar, who is an ideal editor and always responsible for the readable parts of my books anyway.

Fortunately, I can develop and test all my inchoate ideas about labor and educational issues with a warmly supportive family. Their experience includes considerable knowledge about art, music, poetry, teaching from preschool to graduate school, business startup and production, sales and service, office management, organizing, truck driving, wine making, and health care, along with all the complexities of going to college, leaving college, going back to college, and completing several different colleges in different locations. When I get discouraged, I can think first of the great spirit of my father-in-law, Gene Logan, who had multiple degrees, careers, and talents and made amazing art until the day he died. As always, I rely more than anything on my wife, Diane Logan Watkins, and my son and daughter-in-law, Christopher Watkins and Amy Marinelli.

CHAPTER 1

We're Going to the Show

The current truism suggests that an undergraduate degree is today's equivalent to a high-school diploma a couple of generations earlier. Undergraduates at a research university would probably not recognize themselves reflected in any historical mirror of high-school vocational education, though, which was a significant source for many of those high-school degrees in the past. Few would even recognize the term "vocational education" as having designated a specific secondary-school track, let alone recognize the derogatory "voc ed" that was used so commonly half a century ago. All kinds of existing cultural pressures teach an enormous range of students to look "up" rather than "down" an educational social scale: at advanced placement (AP) courses in high school, at a prestigious university or professional school down the line, and so on. Obviously, not all students absorb these directional lessons, but it seems clear enough that in educational terms the eyes-up injunction rules the day, arguably in more intense and comprehensive ways than in the very recent past. Educational institutions may seem shaped in direct relation to academic ends or programmatic goals. In the apparently endless competition of the present, however, what is directly above on the escalator always matters, what is directly above is itself defined by the next level, and so on through the process.

Nevertheless, there are good reasons to change this angle of vision. The range and diversity of postsecondary education in the United States today can be better understood in the historical mirror of vocational education than by looking up the educational escalator.

Of course, "getting ahead" has always seemed a part of cultural common sense in this country, and you cannot get ahead unless you look higher than where you are. From Benjamin Franklin through Frederick

Douglass and on into the twentieth century, the idea of having to beat the odds emerged as a decided part of achieving whatever success you wanted. As both Franklin and Douglass remind us often, a clear awareness of the odds as stacked against you is a useful spur, a way of keeping yourself focused on your goals and working harder to achieve them. Later, the Horatio Alger stories kept the odds (or at least the appearance of odds) and the hard-work parts, but they typically added a benefactor and various other external elements that fudged the purity of "self-made man" concepts. As Bruce Robbins explains in *Upward Mobility and the Common Good*, benefactors are actually integral to upward mobility stories in all kinds of ways. Robbins also reminds us that, contrary to the clichés about Alger, his stories are not really rags-to-riches success epics. Far more typical is the achievement of a kind of solid middle-class respectability and financial security. Dick and the rest of the crew do not aspire to challenging a gilded elite for the crown of wealthiest. Hard work (and often a benefactor or so) let you beat the odds and settle into the decent rewards of a good life.

By the mid-twentieth century westerns often served as obvious examples of the persistence of these against-all-odds plots. Even when relatively complicated by other elements, such as in *High Noon* in 1952, the basic against-all-odds plot links everything up. Just in case we missed the point, the early bar conversation among the townspeople in *High Noon* reminds us that Marshal Will Kane (Gary Cooper) probably won't last five minutes after the arrival of the outlaw Frank Miller (Ian MacDonald). The good marshal looks to be in for a difficult time even before we know the exact odds he faces as more and more townspeople desert his cause.

Initially, vocational education seems a very curious mirror to hold up to the continuing story of these against-all-odds expectations and the promises of getting ahead, because vocational education was not really conceived as a way for people to get ahead at all. Early in the twentieth century, major figures in education such as John Dewey were often associated with initiatives to begin or expand vocational training in the schools. One of Dewey's central ideas involved the integration of vocational and academic training as part of an ideal of educating the whole person. It was the passage of the Smith-Hughes Act in 1917, however, that supplied not only federal funding but also political legitimacy to public secondary-school programs in vocational training. The terms of Smith-Hughes reflected almost nothing of Dewey's thinking and a great deal of the thinking of a much more obscure figure in educational history, Charles Prosser. Prosser had advanced rapidly in his public career, from president of the

Indiana State Teachers Association to deputy commissioner for vocational education in Massachusetts working under his former Columbia professor of education, David Snedden. By 1912 he had been elected executive secretary of the National Society for the Promotion of Industrial Education, a position that gave him considerable leverage in his successful lobbying for the specific provisions of Smith-Hughes.

In contrast to Dewey's emphasis on integrating all aspects of education, Prosser firmly believed in the separation of vocational training from a general academic education. Certainly the training process as Prosser imagined it would involve considerable hard work on the part of students, and students were to be well prepared for trade and industrial positions that promised some real degree of lifetime stability. But Prosser was adamant that vocational education *not* be defined by some putatively more prestigious academic training, which Prosser often referred to in derogatory terms as little more than an education for "leisure culture." Students were not encouraged to think about "bettering themselves" by progressing beyond the specific jobs for which they had been trained. His conception of vocational education had little to do with any cultural common sense about how to beat the odds for success. Prosser was interested in building a working class to meet the needs of a burgeoning industrial economy, not in contributing to a middle-class mythology of individuals getting ahead.

My primary interest lies less in this early history than in the reform directions that emerged in the 1980s and 1990s and that directly challenged the central elements of the vocational-education system Prosser had been so instrumental in developing. Prosser had understood very well that the successful separation of vocational training depended on other things besides instructor expertise at job-skill training. Until well past the mid-twentieth century, one of his basic assumptions had largely remained in place: that large masses of future laborers had to be psychologically acclimated by their education to accept a working life in a trade or in a relatively low-status job in routinized production. When Burton Clark borrowed the term "cooling out" in 1960 in *The Open-Door College* to describe community-college counseling, a vocational-education track and its counselors had been cooling out students for some time.

In the 1980s and 1990s, Prosser's dual-track system became one of the primary targets for reform. Even more significantly for my purposes, reformers recognized that challenging the separation of tracks also meant a profound change in the kind of cooling-out function that vocational education had performed. Summarily, vocational education went from cooling out expectations to heating up expectations. In 1998 even the name was changed: from the American Vocational Association that had been around since early in the century to the new Association for Career and Technical Education.

This general heating up of vocational expectations has become as functionally necessary to class formation in the present as a cooling out of expectations had been to class formation through much of the twentieth century. Educationally, the making of a working class had been located in a separately identified secondary-school vocational track and strongly linked with the cooling-out process. With the heating up of expectations in contrast, the primary educational location of class formation moves to a much more heterogeneous and shifting ensemble of postsecondary programs and institutions that connects four-year undergraduate programs with community colleges, distance learning, continuing education, certificate programs, tech schools, and online universities. The "voc ed" of the past was immediately identifiable by its separate track status in secondary schools. As the "voc ed" of the present, however, this complex of postsecondary education represents a more complicated ensemble of relations and one that escapes the familiar critique that higher education has now been "vocationalized" in the service of corporate imperatives.

Indeed, it seems to me quite possible to turn that argument around to suggest instead that the reforms of vocational education initiated in the 1980s and 1990s were designed to "academicize" vocational training. Such debates are interesting, but keeping the focus on class formation offers a more comprehensively useful angle of understanding. The reforms aimed at eliminating the separate status of vocational education, the transformation from a cooling out to a heating up of expectations, and the new positioning of that complex of postsecondary education can explain a great deal about the changing directions of class formation in the United States. Conversely, understanding those directions of class formation will help identify how much and in what ways postsecondary educational institutions are changing.

Although they functioned in other connections as well, against-all-odds plots were often crucial to getting-ahead stories. During the 1980s and 1990s, however, something began happening to these plots. For one thing, they proliferated, seeming to appear everywhere and to apply to virtually anything. I was reminded of how strongly that proliferating tendency continues by a sign in one of our local grocery stores. The sign explains the virtues of self-checkout by suggesting that it is how you "beat the odds" of long waits in checkout lines. In a similar way, Caltrans solicits freeway commuters in the San Francisco Bay area to purchase a FasTrak transponder in order to use special freeway lanes on the bridges and beat the odds of traffic jams. Film and TV thrive on against-all-odds plots. Superheroes by the dozen save various sorts of planets and things day in and day out against all odds, though one does wonder what exactly the point of having a superpower might be if one still must face impossibly difficult odds of success each time. It's not just superheroes or action heroes by any means, however, for even the most mundane stuff on screen longer than a minute or so seems caught up in the same against-the-odds drama. Every other TV commercial seems to feature a hopelessly lumpy, pasty-faced guy somehow (against all odds to be sure) linked with an impossibly beautiful and intelligent woman. People have a lifetime of fun in every car commercial just because the model they've chosen beats the odds of boredom attendant on every other possible model—and, incidentally, does its part for the environment. And then there's *National Review* editor Kathryn Jean Lopez's recent idea for a really good new kind of Hollywood film that appeared in her column on July 27, 2007, in the *Sacramento Bee*. It would be entitled *Power to the People!*, and the plot would be very simple: "A group of media conservatives helps kill a bad bill against all odds."

These plots not only proliferate but also repeat—and repeat and repeat. Video games are perhaps the obvious example here. Typically, the higher the level the more stacked the odds against you, but then you can try it over and over. If you miss whatever Will Kane–Frank Miller equivalent the first time, you can do it again. Or, if you're not a gamer, you can still plan on hitting the rerun, sequel, or remake of a favorite film or show via DVD and TiVo. Frederick Douglass, one remembers, like Benjamin Franklin before him and Horatio Alger and any number of others after him, looked to steep odds as an incentive. You knew you had to keep focused and work as hard as possible because the odds for success were stacked against you. You may be scared, like Will Kane, but after all, this was the arc of an entire lifetime at stake, not a mere one-off occasion admitting do-overs.

But against-all-odds plots seem not to be against much of anything these days. They are a cultural commonplace, hardly remarkable in any context.

It is tempting, then, to worry the decline of hard work as a virtue or the trivializing of lifetime decisions or media-induced short attention spans or whatever. I think it more likely, however, that the leverage supplied by an against-all-odds incentive in those earlier getting-ahead narratives might seem to have disappeared only because against-all-odds plots now largely do some other kind of cultural work. Student response is as good an indicator as anything that the game has changed. My undergraduates usually seem aware enough that a great many of the cultural texts and visuals around them turn on a basic against-all-odds plot. Occasionally, some will think themselves too sophisticated to identify with the central character on screen in film or game, yet when we talk about against-all-odds plots in class, most of my students are willing to admit that the central figure who succeeds against the odds is a desirable mirror. Regardless, nobody identifies with the mass of characters whose sole purpose is to establish that there are "odds" in the first place. The (usually rapid) deaths, disfigurements, disgraces—whatever—of these filler characters graphically demonstrate how centrally heroic our central character really is, given that such odds exist against success. The July 13, 2007, issue of *Entertainment Weekly* reported that in films opening that year between May 4 and July 4 at over a thousand screens, the body count stood at 17,014. At a good guess, few if any in any audience related to or identified with any of the dead.

Nevertheless, against-all-odds plots have become so pervasive that even when pushed to think about the sheer weirdness of sitting in front of a screen like millions of others, all identifying with the character who succeeds against all odds, my students find it nearly impossible to imagine much by way of any other kind of narrative—at least of their preferred kind, where one is invited to "relate to" or "identify with" the characters. The simplest connection to my argument is that the continual heating up of expectations requires continual intensification. Thus, rather than the traditional incentive to hard work, the against-all-odds plot supplies a necessary accelerator for the heating-up process. Across the endless identity representations made endlessly available, the process of relating to or identifying with this one or that one against the odds is what turns up the heat. Which is not quite the same "identity" as that classic Gary Cooper sense of the kind of marshal, indeed the kind of person he has been all his life, and so of necessity he must stay an extra day at least to try to shoot Frank Miller dead, as the soundtrack conveniently explains. Unlike the incentive to work hard to overcome odds or the internalized identity thematics running through the Marshall's mind, here it is the *positioning* as against all the odds that matters first. For no matter what exactly the odds or the specific character traits or the twists and turns of plot or the relative seriousness or triviality of the occasion, it is the fact of being positioned against the odds that brings the necessary individuation and special uniqueness of "the one." Thus, each time the position can be occupied, even in the most trivial of circumstances, the process raises expectations for the next time and the next, ensuring that, among other things, there must always be a "next."

My more specific puzzle, however, lies right behind that simple general connection: namely, the incorporation of vocational education into this continually accelerating heating up. Reform initiatives certainly seemed headed in the direction of including vocational training within a vision of educational change. The first comprehensive legislation regarding vocational education since Smith-Hughes in 1917 had been passed in 1963, and it already signaled some considerable disillusion with the relevance of Prosserized ideas for current circumstances of vocational training. The career-education movement of the 1970s was short-lived as a federal government policy priority, but its visibility heralded the emergence of profound revisions of the basic assumptions that had informed Prosser's original conception. Vocational education as the voc ed of ill repute did not disappear with the advent of career-education thinking by any means. But by the end of the 1980s, the so-called new economy was well into gear, and the issue of workforce training became central to any number of reform initiatives across a wide range of the political spectrum. Massive economic changes on the horizon meant that the educational system as a whole would require the same kind of comprehensive overhaul that had marked the early twentieth century, only this time in the service of postindustrial labor requirements. Fueled by the appointment of prestigious commissions such as the Secretary's Commission on Achieving Necessary Skills that produced the SCANS guidelines with Department of Labor sponsorship, and by reports such as *America's Choice: High Skills or Low Wages!* from the National Center on Education and the Economy, educational reform became an economic concern.

The new economy would need "smart workers" habituated to the accelerating flood of technological development and, even more importantly, empowered by their educations to welcome innovation and change. Flexibly organized workplace teams would replace static hierarchies of labor demarcations, and a lifelong commitment to continual educational retooling would replace the idea of specific qualifications for an already determined labor slot. Above all, students would come to share an assumption that their individual decisions about every level of production and marketing would have real effects on outcomes. As a result, vocational-education students could no longer be trained to become the habit-driven behavioral switchboards Prosser had imagined. Vocational students would become full-fledged members of a choice economy, where every choice ups the ante for the next. For the first time vocational students would no longer be the extras hired to get killed in the first ten minutes or who remain invisibly working in the scene rooms offscreen. They would be encouraged to join everybody else in the theater in seeing themselves in the hero of the against-all-odds plot.

The idea so often expressed in reform initiatives—that a new economy would simultaneously democratize the workplace and empower everyone inclusively as democratic citizens—is likely to appear little more than a fantasy at best from the perspective of a post-9/11 world during the convulsions of the Bush regime. Nevertheless, I think it significant that nothing has emerged within vocational training that would serve to restore its cooling-out function. Despite all the signs of "lowered expectations," no massive institutional force is positioned to do the lowering, as vocational education had been in the past.

True to the dynamics of current against-all-odds plots, any lowering that goes on always applies to someone else. The accelerators continue, with the expectations that everyone must learn to *choose* success and endlessly compete to beat the odds. Prosser had assumed that for the students in vocational education choices were necessarily constrained to the conditions of their training. In these new circumstances, however, choice becomes the primary ideological category of exchange, and the reasons for the incorporation of vocational education students within the heating up required of a choice economy have everything to do with this shift in the processes of class formation.

Historically, class formation has always functioned importantly in the organization of vocational training, and I will argue that class formation continues to be crucial even in these new conditions involving the centrality of choice and the heating up of expectations. We must also recognize, however, that the decline of vocational education as a separate secondary-school track coincides roughly with the period in which the very idea of "class" came under scrutiny in new ways. So successful was Reaganism in the United States and Thatcherism in Britain that even left theorists began considering class an obsolete category. Ernesto Laclau and Chantal Mouffe, for example, argued throughout their book *Hegemony and Socialist Strategy* (1985) that the possibility had to be faced that class analysis was born in another age and had now lost its usefulness to understand the specific complexities of the present. In response to many such critiques, class analysis all too often became simply an idea to defend rather than something to use.

While not pretending resolutions to these complex debates, my focus on vocational reforms affords a productive angle to explore some alternative directions. I would hardly want to pursue the connection to the point of arguing that the putative "disappearance of class" and the reform dream of a "disappearance of voc ed" as a segregated track pose exactly the same set of questions. Nevertheless, it is a doubly useful coincidence for my purposes.

Class processes change, and rather than arrive at the comfortable conclusion that class is obsolete, understanding more about the vocational education reforms in the 1980s and 1990s can help explain something about the direction and momentum of change. At the least, thinking by way of vocational education reforms should offer some relief from the apparently interminable debates about economics and culture. Vocational education was always the educational sector tied most closely to the economy of labor and to workplace relationships, and in its inception, as I have already suggested, directly represented as central to a process of working-class formation. Yet in all its various forms it was also an educational project, and hence deeply involved in an entire ensemble of cultural operations. Before postmodernism supposedly collapsed the boundaries of culture and the economy, vocational education striated a complex field of constantly overlapping intersections among multiple economic and cultural elements.

Over its long history through the twentieth century, part of everyday classroom training for countless students involved learning the necessary daily negotiations that would continue to organize their working lives. Acquiring the skills of construction welding might well include, for example, an economic lesson in understanding that trade's utility to specific industries and the often geographically determined differences among industry practices in specific locations; a political lesson in understanding the regulatory powers that established the standards for work in the trade; a cultural lesson in the skills of reading, from shop manuals to ways of understanding how best to represent oneself to a potential employer; and, finally, a rhetorical lesson in persuasion, how to convert the cultural means of representing an economically viable skill into an actual salary in a specific job. Prosser had insisted on teaching only those things directly linked to necessary job skills, but over the decades the definitions of "necessary" turned out to be quite elastic.

Turning the connection the other way, class analysis offers a means of recognizing larger issues at stake in the reform initiatives of the 1980s and 1990s. Like the against-all-odds plot, the heating up of expectations from vocational training can suggest a trick. It seems simply an expansion of the long-familiar educational ideology of false promises that has now become so much an institutional and perceptual norm that it is only barely recognizable as either false or ideological. But like all such accounts that depend too much on the assumption of a great many stupid people, this explanation finally is not very explanatory. The heating up of expectations involves considerably more than simply a glittering promise that deceives people. It involves a shift in processes of class formation. Richard Wolff and Stephen Resnick's *Knowledge and Class*, published in 1987, roughly the middle of the reform period of vocational training, offers an exception to the general absence of theorizing about class. They developed powerful ways of understanding class around the idea of class processes rather than group identity or the more sociologically inflected conception of aggregate groups of similarly positioned individuals. Although I am not entirely in agreement with their arguments, I will emphasize often in this book the idea of class processes as particularly useful in understanding this recent shift in class formation marked by the transformation of vocational education.

How do you build selves immediately responsive to the heating up of expectations in an imaginary of individual choice as everywhere, saturating everything? Before turning more directly to vocational education reform initiatives in chapter 3, I want to explore this question in the next chapter by juxtaposing the ideas of class inclusiveness that emerge in educational reform to a very different discourse of class that emerged in reaction to the successes of Reaganism. Left critics have often maintained that dominant U.S. ideologies engage in what George Lipsitz refers to as "our society's erasure of class" (1997, 10) and certainly the erasure of class analysis in anything like the Marxist sense Lipsitz describes. Nevertheless, a *terminology* of class remains an often almost obsessive point of reference, especially the idea of being middle class. Nowhere has middle-classness been so relentlessly universalized as in the United States, not by claiming to be the heir to glorious civilizations in the past, but rather by spilling tapestries of detail in every possible direction and proclaiming the potential availability of a middle-class life as the appropriate mirror for everyone.

Alan Wolfe, for example, could begin *One Nation After All*, his report on his Middle Class Morality Project, with statistics drawn from the General Social Survey showing that "at no time between 1972 and 1994 did more than 10 percent of the American population classify themselves as *either* lower class or upper class" (1998, 1; Wolfe's emphasis). Any term stretching across such a population range seems empty of content, and the very idea of such a Middle Class Morality Project sounds like little more than the continuation of a popular strategy of the "social issues" right beginning well before the Reagan years. Once put in place to identify a general, normative consensus, "middle class" then becomes available to measure whatever range of deviation one perceives as looming dangerously on the horizon. Wolfe's argument was intended as a polemical intervention in the face of a new set of concerns that had emerged in the 1980s and 1990s, a deeply pessimistic thematics of middle-class decline and disintegration as a result of Reaganism.

Under his ascendant conservatism, these critiques argued, the federal government had been recast in the evil image of "the Welfare State," forever interfering with normal, healthy social and economic processes and hence something to be dismantled wherever and whenever possible. Other institutions, in particular schools and workplaces, were pressured to redesign toward the ends of maximizing corporate and military imperatives rather than serve as the necessary framework of individual democratic citizens. With little left of state authority to redress the historical effects of political exclusions or to ameliorate the negative effects on individuals of massive forces at work such as the competitive intensities of a marketplace economy, more and more individuals were simply cast aside with no chance of a future middle-class life. Reaganism had put the squeeze on the middle class, thereby escalating a polarization of top and bottom.

By the end of his book even Wolfe evidences some considerable worry about the future of a middle class in the United States. His Irving Kristol–like closing admonition seems in many ways closer to liberal Robert Reich's warning in *The Work of Nations* at the beginning of the decade than to the hymns of capitalist triumphalism more typically emanating from the right: "The upper-class withdrawal syndrome is truly to be feared. It would be ironic indeed if the middle-class ideal of one nation survived the left's romanticism only to fall victim to the right's cynicism" (1998, 322).

Against such considerable and widespread concern about middle-class decline, it is initially hard to explain the optimism of typically no less liberal groups of vocational education reformers in looking at the "same" economy as full of promise for the future rather than the enemy at now unprotected gates. Vocational education reformers, however, were more immediately interested in the kind of workplaces and workplace relations emerging in a new economy than in the macro relation of the economy to the state. Given the new organizational flexibilities and the obsolescence of rigid hierarchies emerging in more and more industries, every worker would have some considerable say in decision-making processes required by the onetime customized product runs that were replacing standardized mass production. The workplace itself was thus perceived as having the potential to be a model for a more genuinely inclusive citizen politics rather than one of the most rigid sources of exclusion and inequality. An inclusive middle-class dream could reemerge in these profoundly altered circumstances of a postindustrial economy, by cutting across the contradictions that had riven the industrial age.

Economic conditions look so different across these contemporaneous discourses, I will argue, because the individual imagined in vocational education reform as occupying those new workplaces is understood in very different terms than the isolated and beleaguered figure that appears so often in the discourses of middle-class decline. Living in a world shaped by Reaganism and its unfettered capitalist expansion, individuals in a declining middle class find their choices more and more constrained. Like Marshal Kane in *High Noon*, they have been deserted by the society they inhabit and have no real choice at all but to go it alone. In contrast, to the extent that future smart workers could be educated to mirror the ideal self of new vocational-education programs, they would seem to have grown up within the endlessly replicable identities in all those new versions of against-all-odds plots, saturated with choices and expecting more and more to come. It is as if they were built and educated from the beginning to be at once continually changing and yet always available as an inexhaustible resource for changing forms of production in the new workplaces they are to inhabit. Responding in *Multitude* to a frequent criticism of their earlier argument in *Empire*, Michael Hardt and Antonio Negri attempted to distance themselves completely from such 1990s optimism about a new economy: "Our notion of immaterial labor should not be confused with the utopian dreams in the 1990s of a 'new economy' that, largely through technological innovations, globalization, and rising stock markets, was thought by some to have made all work interesting and satisfying, democratized wealth, and banished recessions to the past" (2000, 111). Nevertheless, as I will suggest, the selves imagined in reform discourse have a great deal in common with those flexible identities Hardt and Negri describe, all inhabiting institutions whose very boundary lines are becoming increasingly fluid.

Indeed, vocational-training reform initiatives often focused on eliminating the barriers Prosser had helped establish between vocational and academic tracks, and in even larger terms on closing the division between work and school. As their names suggest, the training programs I will discuss in chapter 3, among them Tech Prep and School-to-Work, feature classrooms that seem designed to reproduce the workplace as closely as possible. Unlike more traditional vocational education programs in the past, however, both Tech Prep and School-to-Work recognize a crucial reciprocity involved. If on one hand classroom exercises simulate work experiences, on the other the workplace begins to be understood first in educational terms. The workplace is a place for lifelong education for workers who understand that constantly changing technologies and markets require continual retooling of expertise. More experimental reform initiatives went even farther, emphasizing *how* to learn rather than direct skill training. While programs such as Tech Prep seemed belatedly to catch up to the central symbolic importance the idea of a "career" had had in the middle-class imagination, these reforms in contrast built into the training process the importance of job mobility. If one knew how to learn, it would be possible to assimilate new skills very quickly on any job as one moved around.

Yet even at the height of enthusiasm for an unlimited postindustrial future of smart work and smart workers, it seemed obvious to critics that no advance of information age technology could possibly guarantee high level–high reward jobs for everyone. Educators caught in the bind created by both a culture of always rising expectations and reform pressures for intensified skill and academic training across the board were especially wary of "false promises." At the same time, even those who felt it unlikely their students would ever command much in the way of such chosen mobility from one good job to another could not afford not to train students as if they might. As W. Norton Grubb explained in *Working in the Middle*, "The paradox, then, is that even though many jobs will not become high-skilled jobs, educational institutions need to prepare their students as if they will—with the broad range of academic competencies and the

SCANS or generic skills emphasized in many of the current attempts to integrate academic and occupational education" (1996, 234). Although nothing at all can guarantee a high-skill job for students, educators must gamble on the possibility or face the fact that lack of such preparation will doom their students to failure before they have ever had a chance to enter the game. Educators face a representational system where school dropouts and the disenfranchised in every sense are rarely represented directly at all, except when made to appear as if some obscure and now obsolete holdover from a past rapidly receding from view.

The promise of job mobilities and the continual heating up of expectations about jobs hardly signal an end to class divisions. I will argue in chapter 4, however, that they do help reconstruct the images of both work and class to conform much more closely to the dominant dynamics of consumer culture. Job mobility means not only searching for jobs but also dealing with the pressures that come with feeling that one *ought* to be searching. After all, with a little effort a much better deal always seems on the horizon. It is as if the familiar vocational skill manual for job specific training could be replaced as a dominant symbol by something on the order of the *Occupational Outlook Handbook*, designed for searching rather than training. With its Bureau of Labor derived statistics and careful projection of future employment patterns, the *Handbook* might be understood as a kind of Ur-text for a huge literature of the job search in print and online. Endless job searching begins to take on all the familiar affective intensities of going shopping. Yet, like any form of shopping, representations of work as consumption have no place for regulators, only accelerators. Consumption accelerators do not really work by stimulating individual demand or in the endless substitutions of desire as lack. The organizing structure of the *Handbook* helps make it possible to recognize how the reconstruction of training for work into a process of consumption reveals a great deal about the dynamics of consumer culture generally. At the same time, those consumer dynamics can explain how vocational training's accelerated heating up of expectations serves the intensification of competition that identifies dominant class processes.

Like current forms of the against-all-odds plot, the exaggeration of consumption as celebrity culture seems emblematic of an expanded ideology of the individual, a kind of hyperindividualism pushing everything to an extreme. In chapter 5 I will argue that this foregrounding of exaggerated individual agency represents a kind of aftermarket psychological investment for what is better understood as a fundamentally dominant class process. Competition has been assumed constitutively central to familiar ideologies of individualism in the United States, but conceptions of competition depend on the boundedness of the individual entities who compete and the limited field where competition takes place. As class process, a current hyperindividualism requires instead the extensive expansion of competitive boundaries. Theories of globalization often seem to imagine a continually expanding marketplace competitive field, to the point that "the market" encompasses everything. But the intensification of competition I will try to describe involves less the expansion of any single competitive field than the extensive prolongation of field conditions from every direction. The result is that nothing seems available outside of competition, and competition never remains the same.

In these conditions of competition, the freedom promised by the idea of wage labor, of selling one's labor power for a wage, no longer quite suffices. Unlike wage labor, which is limited to work as a distinct social sphere, the generality of choice makes the power to choose seem available to travel anywhere into any sphere. Choice begins to replace the selling of individual labor power as the central ideological building block of a contemporary class formation. What the intensification of competition produces, however, is the residual labor that the foregrounding of choice obscures, as if nothing but a kind of waste labor left behind by competitive processes. Exploitation then becomes a second-order operation whereby labor as waste can be effectively reclaimed as a motor force of labor power for the future. Rather than a direct extortion of surplus labor by the dominant class from the subordinate class, exploitation requires an intermediating middle managerial organization located in the midst of the complex of postsecondary vocational education. I will argue in my concluding chapter that managing educational labor in this new sense has become a primary function of academic work in the humanities.

Sheila Slaughter and Larry Leslie's *Academic Capitalism* (1997) and Slaughter's subsequent book with Gary Rhoades, *Academic Capitalism and the New Economy* (2004), focus predominantly on entrepreneurial research and the rise of the technosciences. This emphasis makes a great deal of sense, since the organizational redistricting leads to a mazy intricacy of patents, intellectual copyrights, subsidies, and funding generally that identify capital intensive programs at work. Correspondingly, undergraduate education receives relatively little attention except to the extent that it is organized already toward the future potential for producing research benefits and insofar as it functions in the immediate present as a source of revenue for what goes on higher up. Upper-level research as textual scholarship in the humanities has seen continually declining capital for some time, however, and academic capitalism will likely continue to accelerate rather than arrest that decline. Increasingly, the humanities are invested in management rather than in cultural capital across a powerful contradiction imposed by the imperatives of class processes.

On one hand, management oversees competitive practices toward the end of separating out the agency of "the winner" from the crowd of losers. On the other, management in this intermediary sense functions crucially in the reclamation of wasted labor. Unlike a reserve army, what I will designate as a kind of waste labor of competition comes highly skilled, with considerable labor time already accumulated. It is and must be very similar to the competitive "success." Thus ideologically, still a third managerial function emerges as the necessity to preserve the emotional intensities of hyperindividualism as a class process. The educational production of skilled labor may require similarities across the board between "winners" and "losers," but these emotional intensities require instead an image of absolute distance between the winner and everyone else, as mediated through elaborate, extended rituals of competition throughout the organizational structure of postsecondary education.

Like everyone, I undoubtedly make as many generalizations about students as I hear from colleagues in the humanities. More often than not, my comments, like those from a lot of others, involve complaints about what students do not know about history, literature, and languages; about their habits with pop culture, new technologies, and so on; about their sense of entitlement as, in effect, consumers buying certain educational goods; about their obsessions over grades, placement, and the like. Fashioning skill sets and building human-capital portfolios while shopping for an education matches up poorly with ideals of "the undergraduate." But even if all these generalizations were roughly true of students, that would at least suggest a reasonably intelligent recognition of where they are: in the midst of twenty-first-century voc ed. If we want better responses, we need first to understand better where they are and what working conditions pressure their academic behaviors. Vocational education and its changes provide the appropriate mirror.

CHAPTER 2

New Selves / Old Selves, Class Dreams / Class Nightmares

Frederick Taylor's story about Schmidt and the pig iron is one of the founding legends of scientific management. It is usually remembered now for the derogatory terms in which Taylor characterized the worker he was looking for and the arrogance with which he went about convincing Schmidt to up his daily quantity of moving ingots of pig iron for Bethlehem Steel—with "no back talk," as Taylor had memorably phrased it (Braverman 1974, 105). It is worth recalling, however, that Taylor began his story with a gesture that would become increasingly familiar over the next few decades of industrial expansion. He explained that he had first isolated and then carefully studied the specific *task* of moving pig iron. From his study he had determined an optimum quantity possible to move in a given period of time, and only then did he go in search of a worker who might be induced to meet his requirements for how the task could best be carried out.

The sequence of Taylor's reasoning bears out the general logic Marx had emphasized half a century earlier. The division of labor in capitalist industrial production is predicated on a conception of the production process as intricately divided into a discrete series of tasks by management, with the end of lowering labor costs and maximizing profit. The division of labor among workers, who does what in the production process, results from the prior study and organization of tasks. Thus Schmidt makes an appearance in Taylor's reasoning only at the end of a long process of study, and "who" he must be is calculated on the basis of what exactly he must do in relation to Taylor's overall knowledge of the organization of tasks in production.

Charles Prosser and other early-twentieth-century advocates of vocational education often had more in common with Taylor than with educational theorists such as John Dewey, who had advocated a form of vocational training in *Democracy and Education* and elsewhere. Dewey conceived of vocational skills as integrated into a total curriculum of study and personal development, while Prosser's thinking more closely mirrored Taylor's emphasis on the requirements of specific jobs. By the second decade of the twentieth century, however, Prosser was already an influential figure in the development of a vocational-education system. Thus, unlike Taylor, who described himself as looking for the appropriate worker, Prosser foresaw vocational education as capable of *producing* the kind of workers appropriate to specific slots in an industrial economy. Published in 1925, shortly after the passage of the Smith-Hughes Act, Prosser and coauthor C. R. Allen's *Vocational Education in a Democracy* set the direction for much of the subsequent growth in vocational education in accordance with Prosser's expectations for training students. By 1938, in "A Forecast and a Prophecy," intended to anticipate the third decade of vocational education and written for Edwin Lee's collection *Objectives and Problems of Vocational Education*, Prosser expressed satisfaction with two decades of rapid growth, but he argued a need for even more exacting uses of the basic principles he had established.

His first principle echoes Taylor's logic directly in its emphasis on studying actual job tasks: "The occupation will be studied to learn what are its demands on workers in skill and knowledge" (409). The purpose of vocational training can then be accomplished more efficiently, as the fifth principle explains: "The teaching content of the school for the occupation will be made up of these demands [on workers] and of the experiences in skill and knowledge—in doing and thinking—which are necessary to prepare the student to meet these demands" (410). The tenth principle marks training boundaries: "As functioning knowledge is what is required, all the knowledge in every field which bears on this occupation will be culled, organized, taught, and used in the training, and only that knowledge. Only the mathematics that is used in this occupation will be taught, and, likewise, only that science and only that drawing will be taught. Similarly, only those 'shop kinks' or 'office kinks' or 'home kinks' or 'farm kinks' [his list mirrors the early occupational groups established for vocational training] that function in the occupation will be taught" (410).

The addition of home economics as a recognizable and funded program had meant that both male and female students were enrolling in large numbers, but Prosser lamented the fact that so few women were enrolled in industrial education, where they could get proper training. "Industry is today no longer exclusively a masculine affair," he argued, "for more than 8,000,000 women are also engaged in productive employments" (396). The psychology of vocational training remained of paramount importance for Prosser, regardless of who is being trained: "The business of vocational education is to help the mental switchboards of pupils to establish good habits in the performance of the work of some occupation. When these habits have been established by training, they will be carried over into the occupation by this automatic switchboard. There is no such thing as a general mental habit, but only special habits of thinking or doing, which this switchboard has built up by repeating them until they become fixed and reliable" (408). The ideas may be more sophisticated than Taylor's, but he would certainly have understood the logic at work in Prosser's claims.

If we look forward rather than backward to Taylor, however, the contrast could hardly seem more dramatic between this first twenty years of vocational education as reported in the Lee volume and the assumptions at work in the vocational-training reforms initiated in the last decades of the twentieth century. The following is from "The Changing Workplace: New Challenges for Education Policy and Practice," the introductory essay by Lauren Resnick and John Wirt to a volume of essays published in 1996, *Linking School and Work: Roles for Standards and Assessment*. The volume's title seems prosaic enough, but Resnick and Wirt are quite emphatic about the momentous occasion made possible by a rapidly changing economy:

> For the first time since the industrial revolution, the demands being made on the educational system from the perspectives of economic productivity, of democratic citizenship, and of personal fulfillment are convergent. Today's high-performance workplace calls for essentially the same kind of person that Horace Mann and John Dewey sought: someone able to analyze a situation, make reasoned judgments, communicate well, engage with others and reason through differences of opinion, and intelligently employ the complex tools and technologies that can liberate or enslave according to use. What is more, the new workplace calls for people who can learn new skills and knowledge as conditions change—lifelong learners in short. This is, as a result, a moment of extraordinary opportunity in which business, labor, and educational leaders can set a new, common course in which preparation for work and preparation for civic and personal life need no longer be in competition. (10)

Like Prosser, they remain most interested in the kind of worker that should be produced by vocational training; yet the student self they imagine seems as far as possible from Prosser's conception, let alone from the stolid Schmidt as Taylor saw him. Against Prosser's pupil with his or her "mental switchboard" automatically clicking through its job-specific, good-habit-established relays, they imagine instead "essentially the same kind of person that Horace Mann and John Dewey sought"—and, as the description continues, someone who might well seem the ideally informed and critically thinking college freshman finishing his or her honors composition course. Rather than hold routine work habits set in place while young and followed for life, this person is a "lifelong learner" always willing to experiment with something new. In contrast to Prosser's vision of clearly demarcated areas where vocational education has the responsibility to prepare its pupils for a specific role as worker, for Resnick and Wirt preparation as a worker means at the same time preparation for citizenship and realizing the potential for personal fulfillment. All this is to take place against the background of an immense economic transformation rivaling the industrial revolution, offering both a challenge and an opportunity for wholesale educational reform of vocational training.

Not everyone, however, greeted economic changes with the same enthusiasm as vocational education reformers like Resnick and Wirt. Far from the "moment of extraordinary opportunity" Resnick and Wirt perceive, other liberal-minded commentators saw new economic conditions rather more like the hijacking of familiar economic operations by inhabitants of an alien planet:

> The Western financial system is rapidly coming to resemble nothing so much as a vast casino. Every day games are played in this casino that involve sums of money so large that they can't be imagined. At night the games go on at the other side of the world. In the towering office blocks that dominate all the great cities of the world, rooms are full of chain smoking young men all playing these games. Their eyes are fixed on computer screens flickering with changing prices. They play by intercontinental telephone or by tapping electric machines. They are just like gamblers in a casino watching the clicking spin of a silver ball on a roulette wheel and putting their chips on red or black, odd numbers or even ones.

This passage appeared in Susan Strange's *Casino Capitalism*, published in 1986. Frederick Strobel and Wallace Peterson quote it enthusiastically in their apocalyptically titled *The Coming Class War and How to Avoid It* (1999,

31) published just before the turn of the millennium, three years after the Resnick and Wirt volume. Strange's picture of a "casino economy" offers an appropriate emblem for a capitalism run amok, they argue, creating the imminent possibility for revolution. Fears of a potential for "class warfare" had appeared earlier as part of a largely liberal reaction to Reaganism. In "Wages and Jobs: What Is the Public Role?" Margaret Weir reports that under the leadership of Robert Reich as Clinton's new secretary of labor, and with renewed support from union leaders as well, the Labor Department was "in a 'class warfare mode,' in the words of one department official" (296) by 1995, ready to mobilize against the "corporate greed" unleashed by runaway economic interests. During Clinton's reelection campaign, however, she claims that "the Clinton camp rejected this route as too divisive, preferring instead to build the campaign around preserving middle-class entitlements, such as Medicare" (297). Strobel and Peterson's argument is largely about how to ward off the possibility of class warfare, as their title suggests, but they also admit to some puzzlement: "Given the inequities in wealth and income distribution that have developed over the past twenty-five years, the shrinking of the middle class and the growth of the underclass, a key question is this: Why has there not been a major political reaction? a political revolt against these trends? . . . In some respects the situation seems readymade for Marxist-style class warfare to erupt in America, but it has not happened. Why not?" (112–113).

Perhaps predictably, their answer is the misdirection and deception coming from right-wing politicians and corporations, such that people have little sense at all of their true predicament. Yet both the rhetoric and the policy initiatives available in reform arguments for vocational training might have suggested a different or at least more complicated answer. Whatever else it is, reform optimism like Resnick and Wirt's hardly seems a product of Reagan-era lies; neither does the conception of changing workplaces, work practices, and training match up easily with the imperatives of those corporate interests most visibly supportive of Reagan-era politics. Resnick and Wirt recognize quite clearly a latent contradiction between the principle of democratic equality for all and the rigid hierarchies of industrially organized workplaces. Set against the history of vocational education early in the twentieth century and Prosser's arguments for slotting students into an industrial economy, they see the changes bringing about a postindustrial economy as an opportunity to overcome that contradiction. Rather than long for a return to earlier times, they look to the future for even more significant developments. Indeed, some of the reform proposals that appeared in the 1980s and 1990s for democratizing the workplace and workplace education seem considerably more innovative and radical than Strobel and Peterson's classically liberal calls for more government controls and more safeguards to ameliorate the effects of the contradiction between political principles and economics.

At the same time, however, Strobel and Peterson echo a number of other commentators through the 1980s and 1990s with their emphasis on *class* issues, unlike reform discourses where the idea of class often remains little more than a kind of vague ideal of inclusiveness. Despite the history of vocational education, where class and class differences had been signally important issues from early in the twentieth century, it is as if class division is just one of those things to be left behind with the rest of that obsolete structure from the past. Vocational education has always been about producing worker-subjects, however, and the juxtaposition of these optimistic reform discourses with the far more pessimistic focus on middle-class decline seems to me crucial to understanding the imagination of subjectivity at the center of reform efforts. On one hand, as I will elaborate, the contrast can suggest Michael Hardt and Antonio Negri's discussion in *Empire* of the passage from industrial, disciplinary society to what Gilles Deleuze famously called a "society of control." If somewhat belatedly, reformers seem intent on catching up vocational education with the flexible, mobile, fluid subjectivities Hardt and Negri see emerging in a postindustrial economy. Concerns over middle-class decline, in contrast, seem a kind of nostalgically flavored rerun of industrialism, derived from the assumption that Reaganism had dismantled the crucial institutional and government controls painstakingly put in place to make capitalism a benign economic force.

On the other hand, despite the more critical perspective implied by their discussion of how these fluid new selves are shaped in and through a society of control, Hardt and Negri share with vocational-education reformers an assumption that economic changes and changes in the conditions of labor have the potential to make class and class divisions a thing of the past. By continually pointing instead to growing economic inequalities and the closure of upward mobility for larger and larger groups of the population, critics of middle-class decline such as Strobel and Peterson and Robert Reich at least make class issues visibly significant. Rather than present the threat of regression to the class boundaries of the past that they foresee, however, new processes of class formation have emerged within and because of the very conditions Hardt and Negri, like educational reformers, understand as moving beyond class. The worker-subjects imagined as inhabiting new vocational-education programs are not really belated selves finally escaping a time warp as vocational education catches up with other educational institutions, as reformers sometimes seem to suggest. Despite the hopes of reformers, new selves are shaped by processes of class formation every bit as much as the subjects of Prosser's program for an industrial working class.

Throughout the 1990s, liberal critics differed widely about the specifics of fundamental changes in the economy that seemed to have accelerated so dramatically in the previous decade. At the beginning of the 1990s, Reich had emphasized internationalization as the primary feature, thereby anticipating the globalization debates that would become so widespread by 2000 and after. Writing polemically against the popular currents of "Buy American" as well as more technically detailed proposals for protectionist trade policies, Reich had wanted to foreground the importance of a global dispersion of production in post–Bretton Woods economic conditions. Strobel and Peterson, in contrast, see the defining moment of Bretton Woods as laying the groundwork for the "financialization" of capital, by which they mean, crudely, the subordination of production generally to the financial circuits of capital movement. They take their cue from John Maynard Keynes's understated warning in *The General Theory*, which they suggest has come frighteningly true: "Speculators may do no harm as bubbles upon a steady stream of enterprise. But the position is serious when enterprise becomes the bubble on a whirlpool of speculation. When the capital development of a country becomes a byproduct of the activities of a casino, the job is likely to be ill-done" (Strobel and Peterson 1999, 40–41).

Ronald Glassman's more sociologically inflected account, *The New Middle Class and Democracy in a Global Perspective* (1997), agrees in substance with many of Strobel and Peterson's larger claims. But he also offers a relatively more nuanced account of the financialization process that Strobel and Peterson identify as the ultimate source of so many current political problems. His preferred term for the present economic system is "high-tech industrial capitalism," by which he intends to emphasize the continuing importance of industrial production. We may no longer want Model-Ts, he claims, but we still demand industrial goods: "BMWs with in-board computers, 24 values, anti-lock disc brakes, McPherson front suspensions, all-wheel drive, electronic fuel injections, electronic overdrive, turbo-charged acceleration, automatic transmissions, digital dashboard, disc stereo, Dolby FM, and so on" (19). He does not at all deny the emergence of financialization, but, as he points out, "economic history does not begin and end in the 'Anglo-Saxon' nations" (30). Like Reich earlier, he is also interested in foregrounding the dispersal of industrial production. Not only must "someone" somewhere assemble that BMW digital dashboard, but also there are significant differences that can be observed in the *relations* between, broadly, economic and political processes across the many nations that now have significant roles in the operations of both high-tech production and financial markets.

Within the United States it is neither obvious nor even indubitably demonstrable to Glassman that political control is now vested in the hands of those who control financial sectors of corporation, as Strobel and Peterson claim. Recognizable shifts have taken place in the balance of powers among production management, financial controllers, and personnel management, and in turn in the direction of influence corporations exert on government policy decisions. But here as well there are significant differences even across a relatively narrow spectrum of major economic powers such as the United States, Japan, and Germany. More important for Glassman, different sectors within the web of corporate structure have often radically different interests in corporate direction. The results of all these differences and conflicts by no means tend automatically toward a relatively more or less democratic political process. But neither is there some inexorable tide toward a centralization of political control within any group of financial controllers.

Technological changes figure largely in all such accounts. And as one might expect, there is a relatively greater interest in production technologies among those like Glassman who wish to emphasize the continuing importance of industrial goods and relatively more emphasis on communication technologies among those like Strobel and Peterson who describe the information infrastructure of financialization. Reich's special importance in this context lies in his early recognition of continuities within his general category of "routine production" workers. As he points out, not only had the older assembly-line image of routine production already migrated from River Rouge to Malaysia and from cars to semiconductors, but also, equally important, the new technologies so vital for the financial sector had created a need for no less routinized labor such as data entry.

Across these varying accounts, it is possible nevertheless to find one general point of agreement about the overriding importance and value of work for individual citizens. In the midst of explaining their rather technical rationale for a full employment policy, for example, Strobel and Peterson suddenly have recourse to the almost metaphysical language of anthropologist Elliot Liebow in a 1970 *New York Times Magazine* story to emphasize the importance of work and to clinch their own direction of argument: "Work is not only the fundamental condition of human existence, but it is through work . . . that the individual is able to define himself as a full and valued member of society. It is almost impossible to think what it means to be human without thinking of work" (Strobel and Peterson 1999, 139–140). Critics such as Margaret Weir and others might be unlikely to endorse Liebow's language as "realistic" in the way Strobel and Peterson do. But they are no less insistent that the loss of tangible benefits that comes with the shrinking of primary sector jobs is no more important than the diminution of perceived self-worth among middle-class citizens downsized out of their familiar work roles.

This emphasis on the importance of work leads to the uncomfortable realization throughout so many of these discourses that something seems to have changed dramatically about the very nature of the labor process in a contemporary economy. One immediately visible effect appeared as the difficulty of applying long-familiar categorical divisions of labor. Bureau of Labor statistics, as Reich argued at the beginning of the 1990s, had become a nightmare of complexity as empirical descriptions of work practices shift and overlap always more abstract definitions of boundaries. Likewise, to anticipate the subject of the next chapter, would-be educational reformers intent on restructuring the conditions of job training in the schools found themselves on the receiving end of a welter of contradictory input from business leaders. Further, there seemed to be no discernible general patterns of response so that one might anticipate, for example, a rough uniformity among large corporations on one hand or among small businesses on the other. Yet, as Reich had clearly recognized, the problem was larger than a matter of determining appropriate categories for labor practices or anticipating specific new job skill requirements. In particular, his broad category of "symbolic-analyst services" was also an attempt to identify some fundamental new importance to the value of intellectualized labor operations. Reich saw great future potential for the United States to become the primary supplier of global symbolic analyst services, but he also famously argued that far too many who held the most productive and powerful symbolic analyst positions were currently "seceding" from the life of the nation, no longer feeling they had a vital stake in national well-being. Whether attributed ultimately to globalization, financialization, or the broad spectrum of technological developments, the perception was that the conditions of labor for some large percentage of workers seemed to have acquired a significantly new range of meanings.

Educators interested in the reform of vocational training, however, often seemed far less equivocal than Reich about the promise of training "smart workers" for the future. Building on the Total Quality Movement (TQM) begun in the 1980s, for example, Kenneth Gray and Edwin Herr argued in *Workforce Education* (1998) that the turnaround from older Taylorist principles and industrial manufacturing processes had put a premium on smart workers with advanced literacy skills, just the sort of worker Reich describes as a supplier of symbolic-analyst services: "As a result of this change in management philosophy form the Taylorist top-down to the Demingist TQM bottom-up approach, the workplace, particularly in manufacturing, has changed. To be successful, high-skills/high-wage workers are expected to have an expanded set of new skills referred to in this book as 'advanced workplace literary skills'" (184). The comparison to an older industrial economy serves as the most frequent emblem of why educational transformation is necessary, and Marc Tucker's essay in the Resnick and Wirt collection, "Skills Standards, Qualifications Systems, and the American Workforce," marked the contrast even more dramatically than Gray and Herr. Speaking of industrial manufacturing, he claims, "A seventh- or eighth-grade level of literacy and a day or two of skill training on the job would suffice for a lifetime of work. Front-line workers were not meant to think but rather to do exactly as they were told" (23–24).

Tucker was one of the authors of the National Center on Education and the Economy volume *America's Choice: High Skills or Low Wages!* (1990), and his larger political conclusions are never far from his arguments about the necessity for educational change in relation to new economic conditions: "Until now, the schools have been organized not to get everyone to a high standard but rather to sort the many youngsters who would need no more than an eighth-grade level of general literacy from the lucky few who would hold responsible positions and require strong skills. But in the modern world, that approach not only patently disenfranchises those without skills but also robs our society of the workforce we will need to maintain the nation's standard of living" (34). Conservative critics had challenged the idea of getting everyone to a high standard as little more than a facade for typical liberal feel-good politics, but Tucker's argument suggests that conservative critique should itself be understood as fundamentally ideological. The conservative assumption of a hierarchy of inherent abilities among students appeared to Tucker as a direct reflection of the Taylorized conditions of industrial production. Given a labor market that required relatively few high-skill workers, it could seem natural enough that educational assessment practices yielded relatively few students with exceptional abilities. On inspection, the "natural" is revealed to be nothing more than a set of conditions specific to a particular form of production in the past. Conservative ideology perpetuates these conditions of an industrial economy into present circumstances where they become both an economic liability and an antidemocratic form of political elitism.

Tucker's specific interest is in standardized testing programs, and while his argument acknowledged familiar left critiques of built-in cultural biases against particular groups, he wanted to call attention to other issues as well. Testing, he argued, assumes a fixed core of ability apart from students' specific, learned academic skills and irrespective of their cultural background. It purports to measure native individual intelligence, and in the circumstances of rapidly changing economic conditions such an assumption about a permanent identity becomes a distinct liability. Ultimately, testing in these terms realizes a self-fulfilling prophecy: "Scaled scores—the way we currently do it—are an invitation to sort our students from first grade on. The message they send is the expectation that the scores will be distributed along a curve. This means by definition that the system expects a significant number of students to do badly. We know that if that message is sent, a significant number of students will, in fact, do badly, because they are expected to do so" (36). Rather than continue to produce failures, schools must instead maximize the rate of student success to meet the demands of the new economy. The limited job specific skills and general eighth-grade literacy Tucker sees in past vocational training would be replaced by a new set of goals applicable to all students, without assuming in advance some fixed intelligence that might be accessed by testing instruments.

Yet if tests must be designed to measure neither the native ability of individual students nor their competence with a fixed constellation of skills known to be required by specific jobs, then the determination of criteria for success and failure becomes a centrally difficult task. It is little wonder that not only the Resnick and Wirt collection but also a great many other studies included significant attention to how standardized testing might be revised to meet new circumstances. One popular answer involved workplace simulation exercises; to the greatest extent possible, test situations should simulate the actual conditions students might expect in the workplace. Ideally, training in the more traditional vocational-school shop had also been expected to approximate the real skills students would need in specific occupations, but these new exercises and tests differ considerably from earlier practices. Simulation involves the whole ensemble of workplace practices and conditions rather than isolating specific skills.

As Tucker and others often emphasized, in the new economy already acquired skills matter less in the workplace than the ability to learn new skills continually and the flexibility to determine what skills might be appropriate to always changing conditions. Students must learn to construct themselves to the performative occasion of the simulation rather than assume that a test is designed to measure some fixed, inherent quality of intelligence. Test situations, for example, might divide students into groups, ask each group to decide immediate goals in relation to the overall determinants of outputs, and ask them then to design processes to achieve those goals. What counts is performance on the occasion, with the understanding that test exercises can be repeated with potentially different results each time. As a result, failure is never permanent; success is never the same. Rather than inflexible grids that identify and differentiate students, success and failure are redefined in relation to the specificity of each punctual occasion. The ideally flexible and innovative student selves Tucker imagines hardly seem programmed to fit Prosser's conception of workers who are habit-driven and narrowly trained. They seem much closer to the symbolic analysts Reich described in *The Work of Nations*. Yet it should not be surprising that Tucker, like so many others, found it difficult to spell out exactly what simulation exercises measured, and in what terms. After all, even Reich had a great deal of trouble explaining exactly what it is symbolic analysts actually *do*.

For Michael Hardt and Antonio Negri, however, what Reich struggles to explain are processes that belong within the larger category they, like other Italian theorists, designate as immaterial labor: "Robert Reich calls the kind of immaterial labor involved in computer and communication work 'symbolic-analytical services'—tasks that involve 'problem-solving, problem-identifying, and strategic brokering activities.' This type of labor claims the highest value, and thus Reich identifies it as the key to competition in the new global economy" (2000, 291). The concept of immaterial labor has been one of the most fraught to emerge from *Empire*, a point to which I will return. In this context, however, I am most interested in their account of how "cooperation is completely inherent in the labor itself" rather than dependent on outside intervention: "This fact calls into question the old notion (common to classical and Marxian political economics) by which labor power is conceived as 'variable capital,' that is a force that is activated and made coherent by capital, because the cooperative powers of labor power (particularly immaterial labor) afford labor the power of valorizing itself" (294). These are of course large claims in a context of a Marxian labor theory of value. But without my entering at this point into the complexities of the debate, their argument has a particular relevance to the concerns about middle-class decline among U.S. commentators and critics, even Reich, who seems much more sympathetic to the value of "immaterial" labor than others, such as Strobel and Peterson.

Whether described in terms of the immanence of cooperation as Hardt and Negri argue or in some other way, the problem is that these labor processes seem somehow self-contained and intransitive. There is no necessary carryover, as it were, from the labor itself to some other register of activity or to individual identity as a member of society, which was of particular urgency to critics in the United States. Recall again the extravagance of the Liebow metaphysics adduced by Strobel and Peterson. Work is where "the individual is able to define himself as a full and valued member of society." In contrast to the immanence Hardt and Negri describe, here the importance of work for the individual is assumed to lie precisely in its *transitive* power, the direct carryover from worker to the citizen who is "a full and valued member of society." That is, in this context whatever might be "immaterial" about the process of work must find its ultimate value not in the product of the labor, but rather in the individual's self-identification *as citizen*. Thus, in relation to concerns about labor changes in the midst of middle-class decline, it seems to me that one might translate in something like the following way what Hardt and Negri describe as a kind of self-valorizing power of labor that need not be organized from the outside by capital.

For these liberal critics in the United States, a wide range of labor processes no longer must be "activated and made coherent" by the immaterial identificatory powers of individual political citizenship. Thus, the disturbance they register occurs less in relation to the political economy of labor that interests Hardt and Negri than in relation to the way in which labor in the past had seemed capable of uniting an individual into both worker and citizen. Material labor had required the "activation" available from the immaterial identity of citizenship; that immaterial identity in turn required material labor as its content. Here in contrast, these new processes—however described or explained exactly—seem no longer to require their fulfillment in the figure of the citizen, nor, in turn, does the concept of citizen supply from the outside the necessary valorization of the work process.

Reich's symbolic analysts, who secede from the life of the nation, for example, can be understood in these terms as acting on the intransitive valorizing process of their labor, which makes possible a dislocation from the now at best redundant effort to also define themselves as "full and valued" citizens. Likewise, it is possible to recognize a perception of a similar dislocation among those financial controllers excoriated by Strobel and Peterson, those who engage in the manipulation of currency exchange made possible by post–Bretton Woods conditions and exponentially accelerated by the powers of new communication technologies. Theirs is a labor process that for Strobel and Peterson requires a kind of conceptual override of any citizen-based politics of instituting controls over international financial circuits. For Glassman, the investment in a process of labor such as current corporate financial planning can lead to what he (like Negri and Hardt, if with some considerable difference in emphasis) identifies as a politics of "empire" rather than a citizen politics of democracy. In each case, that is, the perceived intransitive nature of the new labor processes breaks the connection between worker and citizen. Thus, in sum, for liberal critics certain new forms of what Hardt and Negri call immaterial labor have emerged in the conditions of a contemporary global economy that permit a process of valorizing the labor involved on its own terms, without recourse to any transitive link to the value or even the identificatory investment in citizenship.

At the same time, for Strobel and Peterson and a great many other critics it was obvious that there existed a growing number of workers either downsized out of a primary labor market or unable to find employment in anything but a secondary labor market to begin with. Their nominal political status as citizens of a democracy no longer translates back into the kind of work that might permit real economic security, let alone anything that would let them define themselves as "full and valued" members of society. Increasingly, they are simply the losers of a globalized economy, and thereby easy prey for a whole range of extremist positions from Christian fundamentalists to militia groups and ethnic identity purists. An ostensible middle class, for whom worker and citizen are inevitably reciprocal terms, is rapidly disappearing from view in the process. For Strobel and Peterson at least, the potential effect is the apocalypse of class warfare between those "immaterial" laborers who benefit most from the global financialization of capital and the "underclass" members that are left out.

Nevertheless, and despite critiques aimed at growing economic inequities, a whole range of recent economic developments are simply taken for granted in these arguments as not only inevitable, but potentially even beneficial. Clearly Reagan-era policies are viewed as a disaster, but the critique rarely extends further in economic terms at least. As Glassman sums up: "The recent experience with de-control and de-regulation has been disastrous. The collapse of the banks and stock market should serve as a warning that the days of unbridled capitalism are over. [Glassman's book was published in 1997, well before Enron and other "scandals"]. Having asserted this, we wish to make the opposite point: that capitalism, though in some modified form, will be an integral part of the high-technology economy of the future, because capitalism motivates productivity, creativity and efficiency" (23).

It is unlikely that every critic would agree completely with Glassman's assessment. Yet with the exception of Barbara Ehrenreich's *Fear of Falling* (1989), with its considerable contribution to class analysis, liberal finger-pointing typically addressed individual economic excess rather than inherent structural problems. Strobel and Peterson's argument offers a good example: "The business leaders of today, in the main, evidently care little about the state of American business or even American capitalism" (189). And although never quite personified in such a direct way, the target of much of Kevin Phillips's earlier argument in *Arrogant Capital* (1994) is likewise the exercise of political control by "special interest" groups based in the finance sectors of capital. For Glassman as to some extent for Reich, the changing economic conditions of a global capitalism could in fact lead to more democratic political processes rather than the current diminution of democracy. Having described the "secession" of symbolic analysts, Reich's closing plea in *The Work of Nations* nevertheless imagines the possibility of individual symbolic analysts renewing an ethical commitment to the politics of citizenship.

In general, the basic problem is perceived as a matter of how to manage a changing economy successfully, toward the end of a future democratic politics. Reich and others suggested that political processes and institutions simply had not as yet caught up with these radical new developments in the economy, and Reagan-era policies exacerbated the worst potential tendencies. Thus there existed little or no effective checks on those tendencies. The emphasis on political checks and controls accounts in large part for why the solutions for middle class disintegration typically seem couched in already familiar liberal policy recommendations for government action, as for example in Strobel and Peterson's suggested "remedies" for preventing class warfare. The result, however, is an almost inevitable frustration that appears so frequently throughout these critical discourses. Checks and controls, after all, are inevitably reactive, and in the circumstances of a booming new economy of the 1990s it was not easy to make belated reaction seem simultaneously a wave of the future. Equally important, to the extent that these proposals resemble more or less familiar liberal programs from the past, it is also clear that their *meaning* can hardly remain the same in the midst of what is acknowledged to be very different economic circumstances. Strobel and Peterson's call for "a twenty-first century New Deal to rebuild roads, bridges, highways, parks, and water and sanitation systems" (182) may well still be a good idea, but in their argument it clearly originated in a look backward, as a control on the present, rather than as a way of anticipating a new future.

In dramatic contrast to these perceptions of broken connections and concerns about how to arrest the disintegration of a middle class, vocational-education reformers often read future middle-class possibilities into their assumptions about economic change. Thus the frequently reiterated narrative of economic transition and the projection of a postindustrial future as if a literal fact of history might perhaps be better understood as a kind of political allegory whose ultimate subject is the reborn possibility of a genuinely inclusive middle-class society. The frequent critique Resnick and Wirt and other reform-minded educators aim at industrial production could then be resolved into something like the imagery of a dream deferred. The ideal of a prosperous middle-class togetherness and social cohesion ran head-on into the relentlessly stratified sectors of industrial labor organization.

As a result, that middle-class dream was forced to live a displaced exile available only through leisure time and the increasing importance of consumption and consumer "lifestyles." Lacking any basis in the organization of production, however, these broadly cultural circumstances soon enough devolved into the internecine conflicts of the present, visible in everything from the culture wars within educational institutions to the so-called tribal politics of struggles over identity rights. Equally important, economic changes—no matter what their ultimate direction—had resulted through the 1980s in the larger and larger displacement of relatively well paid manufacturing jobs, the continual "downsizing" of jobs on into the 1990s, the much ballyhooed phenomenon of "angry white men" out of work and increasingly violent, and the threat once more of a deep class polarization in the country. As an allegorical sign, the monumental change from an industrial to a postindustrial economy reads finally as an opportunity to do all this history over, and to do it right, to create an inclusive democratic middle class.

Yet the individual self at the center of these optimistic projections seems very different from Strobel and Peterson's account, for example, where one's individual identity as worker and as citizen risks permanent disconnection. In the passage I quoted earlier from Resnick and Wirt's introduction, it is as if (borrowing Hardt and Negri's language again) the potential is there for everything to become "immanently" identified as demands converge: "the demands being made on the educational system from the perspectives of economic productivity, of democratic citizenship, and of personal fulfillment are convergent." In this conception, to be a worker would also and for the same reasons mean to be already a citizen and to realize the potential for personal fulfillment. Nothing need intervene from the outside to establish the nexus of connections. To put it a slightly different way, the self that emerges in an argument like Strobel and Peterson's is clearly linked to their emphasis on work as production, with the workplace as a specific location separated from school, from home, or from the voting booth. In contrast, the worker-citizen-fulfilled self of Resnick and Wirt's projection seems far more at home in the dynamic instabilities of consumer culture where these lines blur and shift continually.

And very much at home in the conditions of simulation testing as described by Tucker and others. The central promise of vocational education in the past had been a kind of long-term investment stability. One invested time in training in job-specific skills in return for an assured career in trade or industry. In this new sense, however, simulation testing functions to link expectations to repeated investments of temporality rather than to the single trajectory of long term temporal stability—rather like a process of shopping with its continual flux and instabilities. Tying expectations to repetition and process thus functions to redefine success and failure as simply part of a series of punctual events rather than the determining moments of future direction. Students were encouraged to attempt simulation exercises that seemed above their abilities, since the only real risk involved was quitting altogether, a kind of ultimate failure to leverage the succession of temporal investments. The assumption was that a succession of performances invariably stretched the self no matter what it was that signaled success or failure on any immediate occasion. Passage, in other words, would depend on temporal investment in the flux of multiple performative occasions across indices of success and failure that only signified punctually, as nodes within the continual movement. Students would not only be encouraged to expect success, as Tucker anticipated, but also, and perhaps more important, to expect repeated opportunities for successful achievement as the payoff for an investment of self. Punctual failure of whatever sort meant simply a matter of "marking time" until the next opportunity arose. As with shoppers in a mall, there is always another exercise, another chance.

In more directly political terms, however, as Tucker's argument often suggests, challenging the hierarchies of intelligence testing might ultimately challenge the grounds for the idea of a natural meritocracy, to be replaced by a far more inclusive and fluid democratic politics. Institutions must then become more flexible as well. Schools should no longer be imagined as a distinct formation that during a designated early period of a person's life functioned among other things to sort out native student abilities and to track each student toward his or her likely permanent slot in a workplace hierarchy. Correlatively, the workplace could be recognized as a kind of classroom, a place for "life long learners" as Resnick and Wirt put it, where innovation and new skills become accepted practice. Having "smart workers" in the workplace means that the job is also and at the same time a process of education. Nevertheless, while the School-to-Work Opportunities Act passed in 1994 had helped make these issues of education for the workplace visible and attracted strong local support in a number of places, the final version was considerably scaled back from the original initiative. Thus enthusiasts such as Lynn Olson in *The School-to-Work Revolution* warned of the dangers of assimilating the proposed changes into already existing programs: "If they are grafted onto existing vocational education—representing a change in name only—we will be worse off than when we started" (1997, 24). Such "grafting" was frequent enough, to be sure, but there were more considerable issues as well, having to do with the effects of reform initiatives that were shifting vocational training toward the production of smart workers and drying up funding support for more traditional programs.

In *Multitude*, responding to frequent critiques of their emphasis on immaterial labor, Michael Hardt and Antonio Negri explain their argument further:

> When we claim that immaterial labor is tending toward the hegemonic position we are not saying that most of the workers in the world today are producing immaterial goods. On the contrary, agricultural labor remains, as it has for centuries, dominant in quantitative terms, and industrial labor has not declined in terms of numbers globally. Immaterial labor constitutes a minority of global labor, and it is concentrated in some of the dominant regions of the globe. Our claim, rather, is that immaterial labor has become *hegemonic in qualitative terms* and has imposed a tendency on other forms of labor and society itself. Immaterial labor, in other words, is today in the same position that industrial labor was 150 years ago, when it accounted for only a small fraction of global production and was concentrated in a small part of the world but nonetheless exerted hegemony over all other forms of production. Just as in that phase all forms of labor and society itself had to industrialize, today labor and society have to informationalize, become intelligent, become communicative, become affective. (2004, 109)

Robert Reich had pointed out, however, that while symbolic-analyst positions may often pay very well indeed, in-person service and routine production workers—his other two general categories of labor—often do not. Given the numbers game that even Hardt and Negri acknowledge, with highly paid immaterial labor a very small minority, the attempt to shift vocational education entirely toward smart workers creates intensely contradictory pressures on educators who teach and administer in these programs, as I will argue in the next chapter.

Hardt and Negri continue to defend their claims by also acknowledging that the hegemony of immaterial labor "does not make all work pleasant or rewarding, nor does it lessen the hierarchy and command in the workplace or the polarization of the labor market. Our notion of immaterial labor should not be confused with the utopian dreams in the 1990s of a 'new economy' that, largely through technological innovations, globalization, and rising stock markets, was thought by some to have made all work interesting and satisfying, democratized wealth, and banished recessions to the pat" (111). Yet the confusion might arguably have some basis with respect to the educational arguments that I have been considering and the kind of student self represented as desirable. Hardt and Negri's account of the transition from industrial to a postindustrial "society of control" in *Empire* often sounds very similar to the accounts one finds in a great many educational reformers, including Resnick and Wirt in the passages I quoted earlier:

> The subjectivities produced in the modern institutions were like the standardized machine parts produced in the mass factory: the inmate, the mother, the worker, the student, and so forth. . . . At a certain point, however, the fixity of these standardized parts, of the identities produced by the institutions, came to pose an obstacle to the further progression toward mobility and flexibility. The passage toward the society of control involves a production of subjectivity that is not fixed in identity but hybrid and modulating. (2000, 331)

This seems very like the kind of subjectivity that Tucker, for example, had argued for in contrasting industrial society with the present as a critique of intelligence testing. Of course, the idea they appropriate from Deleuze of a society of control suggests a considerably more critical perspective than Tucker's, to say the least. Nevertheless, every bit as much as Tucker and many other vocational-education reformers, they see in current economic conditions the potential for bringing an end to invidious political exclusions.

In *Empire* they had argued that the class conflicts that had marked an industrial economy were themselves partial and historically specific versions of the full realization of the proletariat now emerging. In *Multitude*, the argument is pushed further:

> In contrast to the exclusions that characterize the concept of the working class, then, the multitude is an open and expansive concept. The multitude gives the concept of the proletariat its fullest definition as all those who labor and produce under the rule of capital. In order to verify this concept of the multitude and its political project we will have to establish that indeed the differences of kind that used to divide labor no longer apply; in other words, that the conditions exist for the various types of labor to communicate, collaborate, and become common. (107)

The immanence of immaterial labor lays the groundwork for the potential for this "fullest definition" of the proletariat as multitude. In any number of ways the often very vague idea of inclusive middle classness in reform discourses differs significantly from this concept of multitude. For my purposes, however, there is a similar refusal to recognize emergent, new processes of class formation and class division as developing not despite but *because* of the conditions in which educators intent on reforming vocational education saw so much potential.

As I will try to show in the next chapter, developing progressive ideas that escaped what so many educators saw as Prosser's outdated conception of vocational training did not begin to solve the new difficulties that emerged. Despite the claims about new directions, the persistence of a Prosser-shaped program had already helped contribute to powerfully negative perceptions of vocational training. In 1998, delegates to the American Vocational Association (formed in 1925, with Prosser's colleague Edwin Lee as its first president) voted overwhelmingly to change its name to the Association for Career and Technical Education. In *The History and Growth of Vocational Education in America*, Howard Gordon notes one of the primary reasons given for the name change: "Trying to change people's views of the term 'vocational' was ineffective. No matter what was said, 'vocational' was viewed as noncollege-bound training meant for someone else's children" (2003, 69). A second primary reason for the change was the association of "vocational" with obsolete training: "Policymakers, businesspeople, parents, students, educators, and the media generally have a negative opinion about the word 'vocational,' associating the word with outdated or lower-level skills and programs of the past" (ibid.).

At the same time, educational reformers intended new programs as alternatives to a four-year college degree and not simply replications. The central idea of training smart workers for a new economy had somehow to mean something altogether different from the idea of a college education for everyone, and from what Gordon alludes to as intensifying pressures around the importance of a college degree. Yet in the midst of the winner-takes-all culture of the 1980s and 1990s, developing programs to compete directly against the cultural prestige of college and a four-year degree seemed impossible at best, suicidal at worst. Meanwhile, businesses facing changing economic conditions offered often contradictory determinations of what might be considered appropriate training. Suggestions ranged from teaching job-specific skills such as CNC routing, for example, to much more general concepts of teaching how best to learn whatever new skills might become necessary as conditions changed. It had seemed obvious and necessary to vocational educational reformers to challenge the prevailing cultural assumptions that had identified "voc ed" students as fit for voc ed and nothing better, and just as important to challenge Prosser's efficiency conception of the student that had dominated vocational training for so long. For teachers and administrators in the midst of curricular change and constant funding pressures, however, the pessimism of middle-class decline and disintegration could hardly be incomprehensible. While the ideal of revisioning the training of vocational students and educating new, smart, and flexible selves quickly became a core project, in actual educational institutions the question of toward what end proved difficult to answer.

CHAPTER 3

School to Work to School to Work to . . .

Educators have found it difficult to keep up with the intensifying pressures of a winner-takes-all culture. Because very few clear pathways to "winning" exist for most people, secondary-school teachers especially are faced with few options. A teacher can perhaps encourage students' anger at being done in by outside forces in hopes that they will try to change things, or attempt to convince them that they're losers anyway and not to bother, or buy them lottery tickets for high-school graduation, or pass them onto college as the symbolic gateway to a successful career—and then hope for the best. In a book symptomatically entitled *Other Ways to Win: Creating Alternatives for High School Graduates,* Kenneth Gray and Edwin Herr supply statistical data to support the perception of many secondary-school teachers that they are caught in an impossible bind. In the 1995 edition, they report that from the mid-1970s to the mid-1990s the percentage of high-school graduates planning to attend a four-year college or university increased from 63 percent to 84 percent. By far the most common reasons cited for university plans were getting a better job and making more money, and by the 2000 edition they were able to add that 49 percent of college freshmen are already making plans for graduate school. Between 1972 and 1992 in the National Center for Education Statistics study they cite, nearly 50 percent of male high-school graduates and nearly 70 percent of females indicated a desire for professional employment, but such professional-level jobs made up only about 20 percent of existing jobs. Parental pressures on children to aim for a college degree have increased as well, and Gray and Herr's data indicate that the increase is most dramatic among parents with "low-achieving" children. Already in their 1995 edition they were able to report that fully 60 percent of students in the lowest quartile of their high-school class indicated significant parental pressure to get into college. Meanwhile, as vocational training reform advocates often pointed out, well into the 1990s the percentage of high-school graduates who actually completed a four-year degree remained remarkably stable at around 25 percent.

While secondary-school teachers, counselors, and administrators can hardly avoid the expectation of preparing winners, educational history works against their efforts to make good on that promise. In particular, vocational-education programs had functioned in almost the opposite way, to "adjust" the expectation lens down for large groups of the population. Voc ed students knew perfectly well that they had not been tracked into voc ed because they were perceived as winners, soon to depart for the college of their choice. Thus, not surprisingly in current circumstances, statistics indicate that more traditional vocational-education programs have been a dying breed since the 1970s. In their 2000 edition of *Other Ways to Win*, Gray and Herr note that among high-school graduating seniors, "only 5 percent of males and virtually no females (0.3 percent) expected to be employed in craftspersons/trade careers" (7). Most traditional vocational-education programs in high schools and community colleges had been built around a necessity for cooling out student expectations. These programs and the heightened expectations common by the 1990s simply don't go together at all.

As early as 1960, in what soon became an enormously influential argument, Burton Clark had charged in *The Open-Door College: A Case Study* that community colleges systematically engaged in a process of cooling students out. In Clark's original argument, counselors were the primary culprits. By encouraging large numbers of students to recognize the immense difficulties they would face in realizing their hopes for a four-year degree, counselors could shift these students into the terminal vocational programs that increasingly became the core of community-college curricula. In larger terms, Clark suggested, counselors thus enabled community colleges to function as an effective resolution to an otherwise intractable dilemma: on one hand, a culture that encouraged individuals to expect visible success in their careers, and on the other an economic system that afforded relatively few high-level positions.

After nearly four decades of debate following Clark's publication, and in what seemed the vastly different economic circumstances of the 1990s, W. Norton Grubb returned to the issue directly in *Working in the Middle* in 1996. Drawn from a range of statistical data and the results of interviews with students (as well as with counselors and administrators, as Clark had done), his first two points are generally intended to complicate the stark outline of community college function that Clark and his supporters had developed. Thus, for example, he argues that there is no reason to assume automatically, as critics often have, that students attending community college who eventually end up in terminal vocational programs would otherwise have attended four-year institutions. A significant number would likely have ended their education with high school, and arguably for these students a community-college degree or certificate represents a certain heating up rather than cooling out of expectations.

Grubb's final argument is worth quoting in full:

> As Clark (1980) himself has argued [in "The Cooling-Out Function Revisited"], any relatively inegalitarian society that promotes high aspirations among its young people must eventually reconcile the two. If it cannot create more places at the top—and this country has been notably resistant to reducing inequality directly—then it must either reduce aspirations in the "soft" ways associated with cooling-out, providing second-best alternatives to students that seem more attainable and realistic, or it must reduce them in the "hard" ways used in many other countries, for example by using high-stakes exams that deny individuals places in postsecondary programs once and for all. The hard approach may be more efficient, and in some sense more direct and honest, but it is also more brutal, more rigid, more inegalitarian, and more hostile to an ethic of continuous self-improvement. A society with cooling-out may not be the best world we can imagine (a paradise where everyone can realize their highest ambitions would be infinitely preferable) but it is certainly better than the alternatives. (1996, 66).

As is typical with would-be pragmatic assessments, Grubb is quick to label admittedly better alternatives as hopelessly utopian. It is not clear, either, why hard approaches are said to be less egalitarian than soft if the ultimate effects seem very similar. But his defense of cooling out is not at all predicated on the more historically familiar grounds of ideologies of merit. He does not claim that since most individuals are not inherently capable of truly high-level job performance anyway, schools must educate students to accept their own inherent limitations "realistically." His argument is that given a deeply inegalitarian society, educators must do their best to prepare students for what is likely available to them while simultaneously exercising every effort to improve the dignity, respect, and financial rewards available from midlevel jobs especially. The argument would not likely appeal to those interested in a radical educational politics of social change, but it would be a mistake to see Grubb as merely cynical or to dismiss the potentially beneficial (if admittedly limited) effects for students of what he argues. While not often stated so directly and clearly, the rationale he presents has informed decades of considerable teacher effort in vocational-education programs, in often the most difficult and challenging of circumstances and with very little in terms of support from their surrounding culture.

Grubb's defense of cooling out clearly offers a striking contrast to the promise of the high-skills postindustrial workplace that appears in arguments such as Lauren Resnick and John Wirt's, discussed in the preceding chapter. They in fact acknowledge the contradiction that informs Grubb's argument, one between a culture that encourages high aspirations in its youth and an inegalitarian economic structure of labor. But as with so many other potentially troubling issues, they assign the force of the contradiction to the now disappearing organization of industrial production: "Others joined with the democratic theorists to promote education for full personal lives, to encourage the lifelong learning and the capacity to engage with enthusiasm and competence in the multiple pursuits, from parenting to leisure activities, that would fill people's longer and longer lives. But the demands of the growing industrial economy were different. Industrialists called for a large supply of literate but essentially docile factory workers who would accept the boring and sometimes dangerous conditions of industrial production" (9).

William Blank shares Resnick and Wirt's optimism about future directions for vocational-training reform, even the possibility of altering the pervasive assumption that everyone should have a college degree. Anticipating a different set of imperatives in future educational trends, he argues in "Future Perspectives in Vocational Education" that "one of the most significant changes we will see during the next several decades is the gradual reversal of the 'four-year university degree for all' mentality that now pervades our society" (286). Thus he reads Gray and Herr's data, for example, as pointing to "troubling" contradictions that will not permit the four-year-degree mentality to last for much longer. He extends even farther the idea of shifting, fluid job boundaries that Resnick and Wirt suggest: "In other words, the clear distinctions between the duties and competencies of workers in the various traditional vocational fields (agriculture, health, public service, marketing, and so forth) will increasingly blur in the future. We will probably see some combining, renaming, and emerging new fields of specialization within the broader field of vocational education. We may even see these distinct divisions disappear entirely!" (288). The implication is that not only divisions but also hierarchies will disappear: "The role of 'vocational' experiences at the high school level may be to prepare graduates to know how to learn well and how to quickly acquire the technical aspects of any occupation" (288). As workplace conditions change and hierarchies disappear, the four-year university degree for all mentality will soon come to seem a relic.

Optimistic projections like Blank's appear within a rhetoric that shares little if anything with either the positive or negative assessments of vocational training in the past. Clearly the idea of cooling out students has no place in Blank's conception. But it should be equally clear that Blank's endorsement of postsecondary technical training as "a high-prestige option for more youth" (286) is no less distant from older conceptions of preparing students for respected vocational careers. Blank does not simply repeat in a new form the longstanding premise that voc ed should lead students into a "trade" that functions in pretty much the same way as a "profession," only on a lower social frequency. Similar to Resnick and Wirt's vision of the newly democratized workplace, Blank's idea is that work no longer necessarily occurs within the terms of a job or a career at all. Thus he quotes with approval from a 1994 *Fortune* article, William Bridges's "The End of the Job: Seven Rules to Break in a De-Jobbed World": "There still is and will be enormous amounts of work to do, but it is not going to be contained in the familiar envelope we call jobs" (287). The familiarly rigid differentiations and hierarchies of jobs and careers will become a thing of the past.

In the concluding chapter of *Working in the Middle*, Grubb treats such projections with considerable caution. The "most likely future," he argues, "is one in which all three kinds of employment persist." There will be "a considerable amount of relatively unskilled work," whose conditions remain largely "unaffected by any of the shifts to high-skilled employment." And while there may well be some increase in "the kind of flexible, independent work touted by many advocates of the high-skills curriculum and requiring many of the SCANS skills," he suggests that it is also the case that a number of individuals "with moderate (or even high) levels of skills" will remain "fixed in their positions by the immobility associated with contingent work" (234). This caution leads him to a "paradox" that significantly rewrites his own earlier defense of cooling out: "However, a further implication is that all educational institutions, including community colleges and technical institutions, need to continue preparing their students for high-skill jobs because the consequences of being unprepared for such jobs are so dismal; individuals who lack the skills to get jobs in the high-skills end of the market are more likely to spend their lives either in contingent work, unable to make the transition into more permanent positions, or in jobs with relatively lower skills levels, pay, and stability than they expect. The paradox, then, is that even though many jobs will not become high-skilled jobs, educational institutions need to prepare their students as if they will—with the broad range of academic competencies and the SCANS or generic skills emphasized in many of the current attempts to integrate academic and occupational education" (234).

Far from being the best available pragmatic solution in the circumstances, as he had argued earlier, this conclusion implies that whether "soft" or "hard," cooling out is a big mistake. Instead, all educators must do everything possible to prepare all their students for high-skills work. Even if the economic payoff may not be there for a great many, discouraging student expectations would be tantamount to condemning them already to consequences almost too "dismal" to contemplate. Thus, by means of what is on the whole a complicated and carefully nuanced analysis of both midlevel employment opportunities and midlevel educational programs, Grubb nevertheless walks backward into the very cultural pressures he has attempted to keep at arm's length. Vocational educators, his "paradox" implies, now have little choice but to acquiesce to the culturally pervasive heating up of expectations.

It is rarely the case in popular media, however, to find representations of "winning" that are directly dependent on the realization of some exalted social position or even a high-level career. As I suggested earlier, the current against-all-odds plotlines of TV shows and Hollywood films undoubtedly encourage identification with the winner who bucks the odds and not with the fodder that make the odds possible. Yet, rather than up the ante of tangible rewards for his or her success, the often outlandish plot development serves more insistently to valorize what we are supposed to know already: the obvious value of the winner. That is, it does not matter that the "challenge" may on some cool reflection seem utterly absurd. There is little or no purchase derived anyway from maintaining suspense about the eventual outcome, no matter the ostensible odds. What the plot delivers is an intensification of what we are supposed to know to be true from the moment the opening pan settles into close focus. The culturally preferred norm emerges in the identification solicited by the plot structure. You are *already* The One. The typical shower of tangible benefits before the closing credits roll is almost beside the point. Inequality and its crowd of losers become unnecessary to think about anyway, given the inward-directed intensities of that "already."

Such familiar plots can continue to escalate the pressures of a culture of winning because film and TV can largely avoid the specifically economic issues that vocational training had had to deal with on a daily basis—at least until the two decades of reform initiatives that interest me here. In simultaneously transforming and intensifying *economic* expectations from vocational training, reform programs could finally begin to promise something on the order of media culture's "already The One." Rather than function as the brake on the cultural world of endlessly rising expectations, vocational training could become an engine box. If rewritten only slightly, however, Grubb's paradox of vocational preparation nevertheless becomes an appropriate signature for the confluence of a winner-takes-all culture with an intensification of perceived mobility in an economic structure. In these new circumstances of vocational training reform, you must *endlessly* prepare yourself for being the winner you already are, for winners always seem to be where you are not, and wherever you are now isn't for winners.

Around 1970 human nature may not have changed (again), but vocational education did. Typical of significant shifts in policy direction, however, the change was explained in the form of a return to origins. The precursor for the idea of "career education" that Sidney Marland Jr., U.S. Commissioner of Education in 1971, established as his highest priority was understood to be the pre–Smith-Hughes Act early history of vocational training. Nevertheless, as articulated by Kenneth Hoyt, who became director of the Office of Career Education in 1978, career education had a distinctively modern psychological dimension that Cheryl Hogg in "Vocational Education: Past, Present, and Future" neatly summarizes as a focus on "the totality of experiences by which knowledge and attitudes about the self and work are acquired" (14). It is true enough that a psychology of the self was part of those early debates around the establishment of vocational-education programs. But in contrast to this emphasis on the totality of lived experience, it had a decidedly instrumental application.

In what has become a widely accepted account of this early history, John Dewey often appears as the champion of education for the "whole person" whose ideas about vocational education unfortunately lost out to the crude efficiency doctrines and separation of vocational from academic tracks that Prosser and others espoused. Thus in *The History and Growth of Vocational Education in America* (2003), intended as a basic text for teacher-education programs in vocational and technical schools, Howard Gordon offers the following summary of their central tenets: "He [Dewey] stated that the primary purpose of education in the United States was to foster the growth of democratically minded citizens, and Dewey made no distinction in the education of those who would manage the companies and those who worked on the shop floors" (32). Prosser, in contrast, "advocated an indoctrinational approach teaching work values and attitudes; students should learn, without question, the ethical standards of dominant society and the professional ethics of the desired occupational area" (ibid.).

Gordon has to summarize complicated positions very quickly in this passage, and as I emphasized in my introduction undoubtedly there were profoundly significant differences between Dewey's educational philosophy and Prosser's. Yet early-twentieth-century perceptions of Dewey's work were not always keyed to the exemplary egalitarianism that appears in Gordon's retrospective summary. In *The Training of the Urban Working Class*, for example, Paul Violas quotes from the 1901 report of the superintendent of the Chicago school system that managed to position Dewey as an authority for what was already a familiar naturalization of class division. "Our educational scheme must recognize the whole boy and girl," the report states, which seems a cardinal principle of Dewey's. As the argument continues, however, a rather different point emerges: "It must provide work for both hand and head. As Dr. Dewey says, 'The simple fact in the case is that in the great majority of human beings the distinctive intellectual interest is not dominant'" (Violas 1978, 146). Dewey might have been interested enough in the possibility of identifying inherent inclinations and aptitudes, but he hardly shared the fascination with offering naturalistic explanations for why the mass of students to be educated were fit only for the kind of instrumental vocational training Prosser advocated.

Ellwood Cubberley's influential *Changing Conceptions of Education* (1909) was considerably more explicit than the superintendent's report about the class basis for a curriculum of vocational education. Cubberley argued throughout that necessary vocational reform, particularly in large urban school systems, needed to rid itself of "the exceedingly democratic idea that our society is devoid of classes" (56) and begin to construct appropriate educational programs geared to the respective social positions of the different classes. To some very great extent indeed, as Cubberley foresaw, the origins of vocational education had to do with the means for preparing a working class to meet the needs of an industrial economy. Discussion of psychological dimensions evidenced relatively very little concern with "the totality of experiences by which knowledge and attitudes about the self and work are acquired," and a great deal of interest in the identification of low student aptitude for advanced learning and the subsequent preparation of such students for industrial labor.

So, far from marking some return to these early origins and debates, the career-education movement might better be understood as taking its bearings from a rather belated recognition of the contradictory effects of what by the 1970s was a long and complicated history of vocational training in the schools. On one hand, as reformers would subsequently point out, well into the 1990s the number of high-school graduates who actually finished a four-year degree remained below 25 percent. Thus, while middle-class students were imbued with an ambition for college, in fact some form of vocational or technical training was the last form of educational credentialing most received, often as a specific requirement of the jobs they actually held. In other words, by the 1970s vocational education was de facto at least an integral element of a constellation of middle-class behaviors around education, jobs, and careers. On the other hand, existent vocational-training programs inherited from the past were often ill suited to meet the career expectations of these students. In the secondary schools especially, vocational education curricula were still often organized around the broad conception of training laid down by Prosser and Allen's 1925 *Vocational Education in a Democracy*. Certainly by the 1960s and 1970s the occupations Prosser had in mind were not exactly the stuff of middle-class career dreams, nor did the training regime he imagined fit very well with the complex of cultural values that Grubb and others have identified as responsible for the rising tide of expectations for both social prestige and financial rewards from work.

At the theoretical level, in texts such as Donald Super's *Career Education and the Meaning of Work*, the career-education movement thus involved a profound shift in emphasis from Prosser's instrumental psychology of adapting students to available jobs to the questions of why people choose certain careers in the first place and how they advance (or not) in their chosen direction. The emphasis on a student centered "total psychology" of motivation and choice seemed much more in accord with the deeply individualistic assumptions of a middle class culture. Far more significantly, it displaced attention away from what had come to seem the top-down imposition of specific "habits" of thinking that had occupied most of Prosser's attention. Not only could students be encouraged instead to "think for themselves," but thinking *about* oneself also emerged as a crucial imperative in the educational pursuit of an eventual career. The theoretical attention to student psychology flowed over in practice into a refocusing of students' attention on their own interests and capabilities. Career education in effect grafted a curriculum of self-inquiry into the process of vocational training.

As a specific and what Cheryl Hogg refers to as a "hot topic" movement (1999, 14) with a great deal of Federal involvement, career education nevertheless was relatively short-lived. The emphasis on student motivational psychology, self-determination, and goals for long-term choices had to be balanced by the obviously compelling issue Prosser had virtually taken for granted: what exactly is all this educational preparation targeted for? How does it prepare students for a rapidly widening range of jobs? The long-term effects of the career-education movement were considerable, however, especially in relation to the growing population of self-consciously middle-class students (and their parents) for whom Prosser's dual-system division seemed inappropriate. Often these were students who were not obviously bound for a college degree, yet who also felt they had no place in a traditional vocational education curriculum. For the most part, their high-school years were spent in "general education" or "general academic" courses in circumstances where no one seemed entirely sure what that training was supposed to yield in terms of occupation.

Typically, major educational-reform initiatives in the past had been directed toward educationally compensating for social disadvantages or, alternatively, toward ways to provide accelerated programs for fast learners. Beginning roughly with the publication of Dale Parnell's *The Neglected Majority* in 1985, however, these students "in the middle" of the performance curve began to emerge as a significant new focus of attention. The idea of a "neglected majority" had a lot of political currency during the Reagan era, but Parnell's specific interest involved how educational systems might better serve students in the two middle quartiles of high-school classes. As president of the American Association of Junior and Community Colleges during much of the 1980s, Parnell had been instrumental in securing federal funding for programs that combined technical training with basic skills.

Operating on a so-called 2 + 2 model, with two years of secondary and two years of postsecondary work, programs such as the tech prep associate degree (TPAD) could provide students with an alternative to a traditional four-year degree. Tech prep seemed indeed one obvious example of "creating alternatives for high school graduates," to borrow Gray and Herr's phrase. It offered something beyond a high-school diploma that was increasingly perceived as worthless in the current job market. But a tech prep degree also seemed much more readily available to many more people than the narrow track to a traditional four-year degree. Tech prep, in other words, occupied a certain "middle" ground of educational credentialing, as particularly appropriate for those middle quartiles of students who were the subjects of Parnell's concern. It also seemed a way to resolve the divide between a career-education focus on motivation and choice and the carefully directed skill training necessary for specific occupations.

Advocates of "middle"-oriented school reforms such as Dale Parnell and W. Norton Grubb could rightly point to a history of educational-policy neglect of both midlevel students and midlevel employment opportunities. If paradoxically, the reasoning suggested, a set of values grounded in the importance of an available education for everybody found its practical expression in a history of reform initiatives and programs that largely ignored the vast majority of students whose performances left them "in the middle." Teachers, counselors, and administrators were all habituated to identify both slow learners and fast learners and to track them into their curricular slots. The immense numbers of students in the middle, however, by virtue of that position were neither qualified to benefit from accelerated programs nor in need of remediation in any form. Thus, more often than not, they were just left to muddle through the educational system on their own.

In 1992, tech prep advocate Dan Hull was even more emphatic. In his brief "Personal Note" that prefaces the resource manual *Getting Started in Tech Prep*, published in the Tech Prep Resource Series, he begins by pointing out the paucity of actual education available for middle-achieving students: "On average, if you have at least two children, one will not be involved seriously in a high school college-prep program. The current educational offerings usually don't do much for those children who are not proceeding 'full steam ahead' toward a four-year college program. So they are allowed to 'finish school' without a plan—and with minimal requirements in academic subjects. It's no wonder we don't want our own children in this so-called general track. It leads nowhere. I would suggest that kids in general-track programs who drop out of school before graduation may not have lost very much."

Hull's ingenious explanation for why TPAD-structured programs should not be perceived as a form of "tracking" students offers a good example of how a rhetoric of choice and planned preparation could be mobilized around a double objective: "By ninth grade all students would select and enter a structured/prescribed program of study in either college prep or tech prep. This does not mean that students are 'tracked,' because they are permitted to switch from one to another up through eleventh grade without losing significant credit toward high school graduation. Either choice means that they are heading toward a realistic goal; they're not just wandering through school." On one hand, Hull significantly rewrites the social distinction implied by the binary of college prep/voc ed tracks, whose origins extend backward into Prosser's division between academic training for the few and vocational training for the rest. In Hull's argument, following the emphasis of career-education thinking, such tracking mechanisms dissolve into a powerfully psychological distinction between individuals merely "wandering" through school and those instead who are engaged in goal-oriented planning grounded in informed choice.

On the other hand, Hull implies everywhere that the long temporal arc of preparation through the sequenced steps of the program leads to a clear payoff. He claims to answer the question about the ultimate ends of training that proved so difficult for so many educational reformers. Rather than a liability, a "second-best" alternative, Hull thus manages to translate the middle positioning of tech prep between a high-school diploma and a four-year degree into an index of effectiveness for everyone. He ends his brief "personal note" by saying, "This sounds like the type of effective education I would want for my own kids. How about you?" In Hull's reasoning TPAD emerges as the appropriately middle class equivalent of the "effective" vocational training that Prosser had imagined as preparing working-class students for the conditions of the actual jobs they would hold. In contrast to Prosser's top down imposition of "habits," TPAD training maintains a career-education emphasis on the intricacies of student motivation and choice. At the same time, its structure and organization function to orient students toward the circumstances of existent jobs and job conditions.

Yet, despite the high visibility of reform measures such as tech prep, by early in the 1990s no clear policy direction for vocational training had emerged. The dramatic title of the report from the Commission on the Skills of the American Workforce released in 1990, *America's Choice: High Skills or Low Wages,* emphasized the urgency of initiating new training programs. Two years earlier the National Alliance of Business had issued *Shaping Tomorrow's Workforce*, whose conclusions seemed remarkably congruent not only with the commission's findings but also with then Labor Secretary Robert Reich's lobbying for active federal investment in upgrading worker skills. The Clinton administration's proposed Reemployment Act, which would have provided massive support for dislocated workers to reenter the workforce with new skills training, never made it through Congress. The business support implied by the arguments of *Shaping Tomorrow's Workforce* quickly dissolved with the announcement of the nearly $13 billion price tag, and labor leaders attacked the proposed compromise, which would have tapped Trade Adjustment Assistance (TAA) funds that were vital to downsized manufacturing workers. The School-to-Work (STW) Opportunities Act that was finally passed in 1994 seemed at least vaguely true to the "spirit" of high skills retraining, but with considerably less funding and with a much greater emphasis on state and local sponsored initiatives, for which the federal government supplied seed money.

In addition to funding difficulties, tech prep often conflicted with other and similar initiatives such as the School-to-Work program. Both were local initiatives organized around consortia of business, political, and educational leaders, but John Craig, director of the Niagara County Tech Prep Consortium in New York, suggests several reasons for conflict in "The Tech Prep Associate Degree Program": "In some states and regional consortiums across the country, support for TPAD and STW became an issue of turf (regarding funding for programs and services for school districts and colleges) and confused the business community (regarding support and delivery of student services in field trips, mentoring, internships, and curriculum revision activities)." In larger terms, the two programs often represented different political positions: "Both TPAD and STW initiatives vitally depend on business support. But the political climate and party agendas cause local community and collaboration problems for practitioners. TPAD is the Republicans' educational reform platform, while STW is the Democrats' answer to better career education for all students" (138). Further, STW funding was on a diminishing scale. The original bill had provided for only five years of funding, leaving administrators at the end of the decade with no readily available source.

Lower levels of funding, lack of clear policy direction from the top, and conflicts among different programs are nothing new, however, and in many locations tech prep and other programs continued to thrive. The larger difficulties often involved employer expectations from the training, and beyond that the problems employers themselves had in identifying desirable worker qualities in circumstances of often very rapidly changing business conditions, particularly in the midlevel job market. The publication of the Secretary's Commission on Achieving Necessary Skills (SCANS) guidelines at the beginning of the 1990s occurred in the midst of a general concern for upgrading basic, general skills across the labor force. But potential employers were just as likely to despair at their inability to find workers who were trained in intricate and job-specific skills.

Among the many interviews he conducted in the research for *Working in the Middle*, Grubb reports as a typical example the following statement from a manager of electronics technicians for a semiconductor firm: "What we'd really like to have that we can never really find is things that are more or less focused on semiconductor processing. There is no hope of finding somebody out of school who has done anything in plasma processing, or knows what lithography is, or any of the basic diffusion. We actually would have a course for our own technicians where we say, 'This is diffusion, impurities diffusion, sifting solids at different rates at different temperatures,' and [we] start going through and teaching that; 'Here is what plasma etch is, and here is how you create plasma, here is how you set up electric fields to etch.' All that stuff we have to teach on our own because I'm not aware of any college anywhere that we could get qualified students [from]'" (22).

While similar comments could be elicited across a remarkably wide band of employers looking for (and not finding) such very specific skill training in potential employees, Grubb's interviews also point to some striking contradictions around the vexed issue of "what employers want" by way of educational training. "On the one hand," Grubb reports, "employers value highly jobs-specific skills, sometimes too specific to be taught in educational institutions and therefore to be learned on the job." He continues, however, by pointing out that "employers often complain about the lack of general and 'academic' capacities, including the abilities to read, write, and communicate in other ways, and the ability to understand and apply math in unfamiliar settings. Some employers therefore castigate occupational programs for concentrating on specific skills to the detriment of more general or academic capacities" (28). In addition to these demands for general skills and flexibility, his interviews continually turned up expectations for employees possessing more nebulous qualities of motivation, initiative, good judgment, willing attitudes, and interpersonal expertise. Even more nebulously, in the words of a Cincinnati engineering manager,

"We're looking for common sense, which is something schools aren't real good at" (27).

Expectations of more general skill training seem more in line with projections of the future labor market inspired by the SCANS guidelines and the like. Nevertheless, Grubb's reading of the input from those he interviewed suggests reasons for caution about assuming that apparently contradictory messages result simply from the uncertainties about an economy in transition. Grubb points out that "the skills necessary for entry-level employment are much more specific than those required for promotion and positions of increasing responsibility. In our interviews, those individuals who stressed specific skills were more often production-level supervisors, while those emphasizing the lack of more general capacities—common sense, problem-solving, and other higher-order, less specific skills—were more frequently personnel managers and those who viewed the firm from the upper levels in its hierarchy" (29).

That finding assumes a special significance in relation to one of the emergent trends Grubb discusses in his concluding chapter, what he calls the shortened job ladder—that is, "the sequence of jobs of increasing responsibility, and the possibilities for on-the-job learning and higher earnings." So-called flattened management hierarchies in many firms eliminate "layers of supervisory workers that previously represented jobs into which production workers might be promoted" (236). Likewise, the division "into lower-level, temporary employees and more skilled permanent employees with higher prerequisites for hiring . . . also contributes to shorter job-ladders" (236). In other words, while firms may continue to require simultaneously employees with very job-specific skills and employees with more nebulous "higher-order" general skills, no clear pathway exists within the firm from one kind of position to the other. Nor is it necessarily the case, as SCANS guideline projections seem to anticipate, that workers who might be hired on the basis of "higher-order" general skills will themselves be expected to perform those lower-level jobs at the production end of a firm's output. Entry-level employees with no way to rise on the shortened job ladder and temp workers contracted out for the occasion will staff such positions. Further, the instability of any number of companies within conditions of continual buyouts, mergers, and production shifts—often into other countries—means that even "higher" positions are likely to change or disappear overnight.

Circumstances such as the shortened job ladder and the disconnect between personnel management and floor production, however, make Hull's claims for the effectiveness of TPAD training begin to appear already out of date almost by the time his remarks were published in 1992. As Hull explains it, the difference between having a "plan" and merely "wandering" through one's education is that a plan involves a highly sequenced series of steps toward a specific career goal. The educational process of planned preparation mirrors the similarly sequenced steps of a career ladder once one enters the career of one's choice, or perhaps more exactly, extends that career ladder backward into the educational process itself. "By ninth grade," Hull asserts, "all students would select and enter a structured/prescribed program of study in either college prep or tech prep." Yet if, for example, typical entry-level positions rarely lead into a sequence of advancements up a job ladder, then the jump from an entry-level position in one firm to a higher position in another firm can no more mark the culmination of a "plan" than being downsized from a higher position in one firm to an entry-level position in another can mark a plan's failure. Given Hull's terminology, it could as easily be said that one is simply "wandering" from job to job as best one can given the exigencies of the moment.

The problem is that Hull's binary of planning/wandering assumes a career education conception of preparation built on the linkage of a psychology of motivation and choice with the organization of planned educational time toward a future payoff. And while the career-education movement had recognized something of the extent and diversity of student involvement in vocational/technical training programs, the price for that belated recognition was a conception of career and of educational preparation for careers that quickly came to seem belated in relation to changing conditions of employment. The point when programs such as TPAD and STW could finally be mobilized around the means of addressing the perceived needs of a "middle" population of secondary-school students was also the point when the very idea of a "career" with its sequenced steps of advancement seemed to be disappearing from the horizon of the anticipated labor market for students in these programs. The long-range effects of the career-education movement derive from its emphasis on student psychology, choice, and motivation rather than the way it could be translated into specific programs of training such as tech prep.

As I argued in chapter 2, 1990s critics of economic trends such as Kevin Phillips, Frederick Strobel, and Wallace Peterson continually pointed to the dangers involved in a dual shift in the economy from investment to speculation, and from production to financialization. The effects of these shifts, they argued, can be recognized in the emergence of a dangerous psychology of gambling that replaces careful long-term planning. Clearly this passage on which I remarked in chapter 2, from Susan Strange's *Casino Capitalism*, has a special resonance for them: "The Western financial system is rapidly coming to resemble nothing so much as a vast casino. Every day games are played in this casino that involve sums of money so large that they can't be imagined. At night the games go on at the other side of the world. In the towering office blocks that dominate all the great cities of the world, rooms are full of chain smoking young men all playing these games. Their eyes are fixed on computer screens flickering with changing prices. They play by intercontinental telephone or by tapping electric machines. They are just like gamblers in a casino watching the clicking spin of a silver ball on a roulette wheel and putting their chips on red or black, odd numbers or even ones" (Strobel and Peterson 1999, 31).

For Strobel and Peterson, as for Strange herself through most of her argument, the kernel of truth in this wonderfully lurid description lies in the recognition that however different in process, both speculation and financialization sacrifice the necessary long-term, planned investment in production to the purely relational indexes of value that appear in the gamble of the moment. Even if only fanciful, the connection to conceptions of educational preparation helps to foreground the considerably more fraught terms in which Grubb's "paradox" itself seems structured like a fateful gamble on the part of educators. For any given student the chips may have been on the wrong color, but educators cannot not play or encourage their students not to play. The consequences of students not being in the game at all are just too "dismal." As a result, the long-term productive work of education seems sacrificed to a gambler's market built on pure speculation and the deployment of whatever leveraged assets might on the occasion fall on the right place on the wheel.

There are ways in which Hull's description of TPAD suggests a continuation of the sound investment practices Strobel and Peterson would support. Students are encouraged to understand their educational preparation as a process in which one invests the whole of the self ("the totality of experiences by which knowledge and attitudes about the self and work are acquired" to borrow Hogg's phrasing again) in educational training on the assumption of a future return in the form of a rewarding "career." In contrast, the reform directions pointed by William Blank, for example, suggest more congruity with the casino economy Strobel and Peterson would deplore. Rather than escalate some destructive psychology of gambling, however, Blank sees the future as opening new doors of possibility. In the passage quoted earlier, he argues that "the clear distinctions between the duties and competencies of workers in the various traditional vocational fields (agriculture, health, public service, marketing, and so forth) will increasingly blur in the future. We will probably see some combining, renaming, and emerging new fields of specialization within the broader field of vocational education. We may even see these distinct divisions disappear entirely!" (288). A little later, he adds the clincher: "The role of 'vocational' experiences at the high school level may be to prepare graduates to know how to learn well and how to quickly acquire the technical aspects of any occupation" (288).

On its face this might look like a continuation of the long-familiar debate about whether general skills or job-specific skills should be the appropriate focus of educational preparation. It seems more accurate, however, to recognize embedded within the argument a very different conception of the temporality of educational preparation than in Hull's emphasis on the discipline of long-term investment planning. In keeping with the focus of the career-education movement, the immediate material of the process remains the "experiences" of the student subject. Rather than encourage students to invest their experience in the long-term temporality of planning, however, in Blank's vision student educational preparation would be shaped on one hand by the timelessly qualitative measures of "how to learn well," and on the other by the punctual temporality of "how to quickly acquire the technical aspects of any occupation." Preparation, in other words, is not divided across the question of whether general or job-specific skills might yield the greater future payoff. Nor is there any implied assertion of teleological connection. Planning how to learn well is not done in order to invest the planning in any given moment of quick acquisition.

In effect, Blank has walked out of Hull's binary of planning/wandering. Hull's sequenced chronology of planning turns instead into the infinitely extendable still life of knowing how to learn well, while the random movements of wandering are reassembled into the always mobile shifts that allow one to quickly master whatever "technical aspects" any given job location requires. Rather than the long-term temporal regime of the plan, "effective" educational preparation involves students in the process of synchronizing these disparate temporalities around the exercise of choice on the occasion. Choice occurs at the structural node of synchronicity rather than in the teleological determination of a future goal. Preparation in this sense would convert what in critics' eyes appears to be little more than a gambler's psychology into what seems instead the educational venture capital necessary to put one always and immediately at stake in a winning game.

In the world Blank imagines, vocational education trains the student how to reset his or her sights from the disappearing investment potential of long-term careers to the burgeoning wealth always available from speculatively leveraging educational financials to take advantage of the deal of the moment. Students might come to see their preparation as involving a combination of qualitative measures of how to perform learning processes while simultaneously strategizing how to adjust such performances to whatever specific operations might be required by the conditions of a particular job. An assumption of job mobility, in other words, would be built into a process that also emphasized a psychological flexibility of adaptation to the moment. Even the testing of students would have to accommodate these new conditions. As I emphasized in chapter 2, the "real time" of learning obeyed both the punctuality of the moment embodied in the test simulation and an expectation that the *process* of learning had no temporal conclusion comparable to what had been marked in the past by the passage across the dividing line from "school" to "work."

Such emergent concepts of educational preparation seem a long way indeed from the structuring of existent TPAD curricula, for example. Yet, arguably, they are made possible by the same matrix of assumptions that had generated both TPAD and STW programs and that had originated with the shift in emphasis marked out by the career-education movement. Despite all the debate occasioned by the issue of what potential employers wanted from training carried on in the schools, career education was never really oriented directly toward the demands of the labor market. One of the reasons the movement itself seemed so short-lived was that in its inception career education often failed to reckon with a culture where educational credentialing was increasingly seen as a direct pathway to the realization of both economic rewards and social prestige. The trend toward greater integration of general academic training and relatively more specialized curricula involving job-specific skills, however, laid the foundation for programs that could claim to be viable alternatives to a four-year college degree as the only gateway to eventual career success.

Most important, the idea of career education fundamentally transformed vocational education through the recognizable class shift from the education of a working class for industrial labor to the education of a middle class for careers. In so doing, it also altered fundamentally the positioning of students with respect to their future working lives. Vocational education not only had been built on the assumption of class inequalities in early advocates such as Cubberley and Prosser, but also had functioned through much of the twentieth century as a major social brake on the generally rising social expectations encouraged by both public education and media culture. After the initial impact of the career-education movement in the 1970s, however, the mentality of being all middle-class together began to be as pervasive in vocational training as anywhere else in public education. The idea of "career" began to replace the emphasis on trade and specific occupations, and students were encouraged through counseling and otherwise to think of their motivations and choices as the central determinants of direction.

The reform developments in the late 1980s and 1990s, however, did more than simply catch up vocational education to the already institutionalized ways in which other educational sectors struggled to slide around issues of job inequalities especially. When Resnick and Wirt link economic productivity and citizenship to "personal fulfillment" they are not thinking in Prosserized terms of the "fulfillment" to be had from a job well done in the knowledge that on however low a level the work still figured importantly in the overall organization of production. Work *practices* themselves are expected to yield something of the same measure of desire and pleasure available from other areas in one's life. Work would no longer be "work" if by that one means the realm of necessity to which, in Prosser's view at least, one must learn to accommodate oneself in the process of vocational training. In arguments like Blank's, as the career education emphasis on choice and motivation is connected to an understanding of job mobilities and transportable skills, the pleasures available from work begin to resemble more and more the pleasures of *consumption*, with its endless media culture foregrounding of choice.

In the next chapter I turn to the way in which these coordinates of consumer desire function in the social conditions of economic inequalities as they are solicited into play in a work-that-isn't-really-work. It is worth remembering the obvious from the beginning: that work can never quite be just another consumer good on the order of toothpaste or bedroom suites. In relation to strictures such as Strobel and Peterson's about a burgeoning casino economy, Grubb's paradox might itself appear as a fateful gamble, as I suggested. His warning about "dismal consequences," however, also implies a certain return of the repressed in effect, a necessity that assumes the new form of a displaced temporality. For the phrase "dismal consequences" not only gestures toward a range of work practices that offer little by way of economic reward or potential advancement, but it also reintroduces in the present a kind of dead time of work associated with nothing so much as the mechanical "habits" of both mind and body that fill out Prosser's vision of the necessity of labor. Yet, rather than the inevitable lifeworld horizon imposed by external necessity that Prosser imagined for most people, in contemporary circumstances work in this sense exacts the vengeance of a stunningly visible consumer culture on those who can now be identified as out of key with the times, who for whatever reason are unwilling or unable to play in the always accelerating tempos of a newly volatile labor marketplace, who made the "wrong" choices.

If career-education developments enable one to imagine the choice of work and career as on the same plane of freedom as any other consumer choice, the displaced temporality of necessity imposes the simultaneous recognition that in contrast to bedroom suites and the like one cannot choose not to consume work, with all the inequities and hierarchies of labor organization. As with any displacement forcibly reinserted into the now alien landscape of the present, however, the notion of "dismal consequences" does not simply mark the continuation by other means of long-standing conditions of inequality. The barriers Grubb enumerates that prevent escape from dismal consequences can no longer be adequately understood as if constituting a familiarly static and impermeable structuring of closed access. Their new secret will lie in their motility, in a time just appearing to recede forever into the past at the very moment the future closes down somewhere else than where one did not leave quite quickly enough.

CHAPTER 4

How the Inequality Connection Was Timed Out

You need a good camcorder to shoot inequality in consumption. Not only do mobilities of desire keep everything in motion, but also—and equally important—the superimposition of image acceleration over taste fills the screen to the point of overflowing. I love Pierre Bourdieu's *Distinction*, but, after all, its primary target is the distanced still life cherished by academics. That critique will not help much in understanding most sectors of consumption most of the time. I think a better beginning involves a slight modification of Marx's famous formula about things seeming to take on a life of their own as commodities. Here, taste operates in consumption to enable desire to take on a life of its own as a thing—which is not quite the same as investing one's desires in an object of consumption. Commodities, one remembers, assume a life of their own in a way that obscures the complex of social relations involved in the process of production. Desire does not so much obscure social relations as digitalize them, in a way that then permits a constant acceleration, compression, elaboration, and so forth on every click. Tastes change, and everything else is swept right along.

Everyone knows, of course, that not much *really* changes in the world of consumption. There is no mistaking an upscale wannabe's Ford-made Jaguar for a "real" prestige car, and meanwhile there are lots of places that Cavaliers live on out of necessity. It is not at all the case that people are duped into thinking material inequalities of consumption no longer exist. The media is filled with stories every day about how the gap is widening. The operation works like the "you're already a winner" of current against-all-odds plots. "Already a winner" doesn't mean that now, at this point in time, you are the sole winning person with everyone else subordinated to you having conquered the impossible challenge. You still have to do the film, and of course sequel after sequel, competing every which way all the while with everyone else around. You just know stuff along the way, including how all this is far from being anything like what "already a winner" means. Likewise, everyone knows that there are inequalities in consumption, that material realities change slowly if much at all, that taste may be hiding something—that you aren't really the sole winning person with everyone else subordinated. Lifting the veil of ignorance becomes just yesterday's porn, because the process does not function invisibly, any more than futures markets or iPods do, though tastes will of course have changed by the time this book is published.

This is a book about education for work and not about consumption, but it is useful to get at least a quick sketch of how consumption works in order to grasp what is at stake as work becomes consumable. A number of educators, often university professors in the humanities, despise the idea of the student as client or customer because, among other things, it equates school with shopping and, not incidentally, professors with salespeople. Nevertheless, the terminology is everywhere, and it suggests the extent to which consumption has become a normal frame in which to consider educational policy direction and issues. That is not yet the case with work and the world of production, though conceptualizing the *search* for work already functions as if directed toward a consumer client and has for some time. But the school-to-work linkage emphasized everywhere in discourses about the reform of vocational training suggests that one clear avenue of carryover to be explored should involve the imaging of student as consumer, the centrality of choice, and a whole host of other elements involved in consumption generally. "The student," Albert Pautler reminds vocational training reformers, "is the client, the customer, the reason for the educational system" (1999, 294). And students in vocational training must learn the consumer responsibilities that go with choices: "Educators must somehow try to encourage students to be more responsible for their own educational program and their future careers" (ibid.).

Vocational education had a special status in relation to systemic economic inequalities as one of the primary brakes on continually rising social expectations. As far more directly in contact with the world of work than other sectors of education, let alone consumer culture, vocational-education programs could hardly ignore the hierarchical labor ladders of a deeply inegalitarian society. The career-education movement did not completely change all that by itself. It laid the groundwork, however, for the major shift I have been tracing in vocational training from a process of cooling out expectations in direct contrast to most highly visible cultural representations, to a process of heating up economic expectations in ways altogether congruent with the directions of the surrounding consumer world. The shift has made it increasingly difficult to isolate visible economic inequalities as reliable signs of class divisions and conflicts. On the model of consumption I sketched earlier, this does not mean that the material divide between "haves" and "have-nots" is diminishing or even becoming more permeable. If anything, it is getting much worse, in the United States and globally. It does mean that we have to look beyond economic inequalities for an understanding of what the shift has to tell us about how class processes function.

Every two years or so since the late 1940s, the Bureau of Labor Statistics and the U.S. Department of Labor have published an updated *Occupational Outlook Handbook* describing in considerable detail the qualifications required and the outlook for employment in a huge number of occupations in the United States. The occupations, one nongovernmental publisher claims, account "for 7 of every 8 jobs in the economy." The Indianapolis-based house has now turned the *Handbook* itself into a mini-industry. You can get, for example, an "Enhanced" version or an "EZ" version or an "Activities" version that lays out specific practice programs in effect for job hunting. You can take bubble-test versions of the "activities" in your career counselor's office. Various CDs and digital versions of various parts are available. Beyond all that, the literature available online and elsewhere about jobs and job hunting is immense. Like a kind of Ur-text, the *Handbook* has spread everywhere and become such a familiar element in the process of career counseling that it is easy to overlook the significance of how the wealth of job-market information appears.

The statistical data available from the Bureau of Labor Statistics are organized in the *Handbook* to provide some skeletal outline of job requirements, working conditions, salary range, and so on for each occupational category. More important, the *Handbook*, like other sources, is in the business of forecasting job trends, both in terms of overall numerical increases/declines and relative rates of growth. A typical entry in the *Handbook* under the crucial "job outlook" heading begins, with regard to respiratory therapists: "Job opportunities are expected to be very good, especially for respiratory therapists with cardiopulmonary skills or experience working with infants. Employment of respiratory therapists is expected to increase faster than the average for all occupations through the year 2012, because of substantial growth in numbers of the middle-aged and elderly population—a development that will heighten the incidence of cardiopulmonary disease" (2004, 296).

"Correctional officer" is projected as another growth category, but for entirely different reasons: "The need to replace correctional officers who transfer to other occupations, retire, or leave the labor force, coupled with rising employment demand, will generate thousands of job openings each year.... The adoption of mandatory sentence guidelines calling for longer sentences and reduced parole for inmates will continue to spur demand for correctional officers." There is a note of caution, however, to help contextualize the availability of jobs: "In the past, some local and State corrections agencies have experienced difficulty in attracting and keeping qualified applicants, largely due to relatively low salaries and the concentration of jobs in rural locations. This situation is expected to continue" (2004, 340).

In contrast to these projections of growing employment, the prospect for mining engineers appears less favorable: "Employment of mining and geological engineers, including mining safety engineers, is projected to decline through 2012. Most of the industries in which mining engineers are concentrated—such as coal, metal, and copper mining—are expected to experience declines in employment" (2004, 137). Yet all is not entirely gloom. The 1998–1999 edition of the *Handbook* had included much the same summary, followed by the warning that "graduates in mining engineering will face competition despite their low number" (1998, 91). The 2004–2005 edition, however, finds room for hope: "Despite a projected decline in employment, very good employment opportunities are expected in this small occupation. A significant number of mining engineers currently employed are approaching retirement age, which should create some job openings over the 2002–2012 period" (2004, 137). Like any good tip sheet, the *Handbook* must keep on top of current information to make its projections.

Each section continues with further explanation for the projected trends, and these projections are set alongside the relevant information about working conditions, salary, and so forth also supplied by the *Handbook*. The "job outlook" entry, however, introduces a key organizing element in how the range of information can be processed. Like an investment guide for mutual funds, the job-outlook entries suggest a relational calculus of risk and reward applicable to every category of occupation that appears in the *Handbook*. Thus factors such as the probability of increased cardiopulmonary disease in an aging population assume their appropriate role on roughly the same plane of importance as the necessity to reckon on retirements or to plot the long-term movements of the metals markets in assessing what work is available as a mining engineer, or the salary range or location likely to be available for correctional officers, and so on. Each piece of information can be factored into account, and the governing frame supplied by the job outlook entries explains the basis for assessment as the relative risks and rewards that come with any given category.

The point is not to criticize the callousness of treating diseases for the elderly or rising prison populations in such a fashion, but simply to emphasize that the vast multiplicity of occupational categories and data has no overall organizational frame beyond the purely relational indexes of risk and reward. For while the *Handbook* is everywhere about a process of seeking employment, that process itself is never available for representation anywhere in the body of information supplied by the *Handbook*. The surrounding editorial "tips" about getting a job continually point to an ongoing process, but seeking employment is not even a kind of absent center whose gravitational pull orients the actual bands of information. It is simply assumed to be going on outside, in whatever diverse individual ways, while meanwhile the internal logic of risk and reward continues to unfold across the manifold of categories and data.

Equally significant, in making use of the *Handbook*'s information and projections, the job seeker does not articulate a kind of missing link by which that internal logic can be folded into the actual process of searching for employment. In principle, it is each individual job seeker with the most at stake in the process. But the conditions of recourse to the *Handbook* mind their force nevertheless. On one hand, the *Handbook* can be of use in job hunting only as an element from outside the process, which is in part why that process cannot be directly represented inside the text. Indeed, should any specific job seeker begin to suspect that the flow of information is secretly attached already to any determinate itinerary of seeking employment, the usefulness of the *Handbook* would immediately diminish relative to an estimate of one's own individual distance from that itinerary. On the other hand, the *Handbook* is of use only and everywhere relative to the process of *seeking* employment. At the point of asserting the directional orientation of occupational choice, the usefulness of the *Handbook* comes to an abrupt end. Not because one has now chosen a single option among many and hence has no more need of information about other possibilities;

a change of mind might again position other options in view. The usefulness ends insofar as the assertion of direction refuses the internal logic of the *Handbook*'s multiplicity with its relational indexes of risk and reward.

The *Handbook* is not a camcorder, but it does seem to me probably as close as a textual representation can get of the larger process I referred to in chapter 3 as the consumption of work. It exposes the source of the pleasure and "personal fulfillment" that Lauren Resnick and John Wirt attribute to work as more exactly available from the search for work, from shopping in effect that always drives still further consumption. At the same time, that source is never in any way represented directly. I have made the *Handbook* an exemplary instance within the immense literature of occupational information because it is especially scrupulous in its notation of specific barriers to occupational entry. Educational criteria, for example, are emphasized not only with respect to each specific occupation but also as good general indicators of existent barriers in growth areas of occupation. There is little if any overt propaganda on behalf of easy roads to success. For obvious reasons, the *Handbook* is wary about directly articulating more or less tacit social barriers that exist in specific occupations. But it is not necessary to read too carefully between the lines to understand how the *Handbook* description recognizes their existence, especially in race and gender terms.

Thus, in contrast to more upbeat sources, the *Handbook* can hardly be held accountable for disseminating some version of that all too familiar ideology of anyone can be anything you want to be if you just want to bad enough, and so on. "Barriers" is perhaps too strong a term if it implies some absolute impermeability, but occupational requirements are everywhere foregrounded with appropriate emphasis on the recognition of very specific steps that must be taken. Likewise, no occupation comes mantled in a sky's-the-limit promise. Specific limits and barriers are marked everywhere, and given the exhaustiveness of comparative data across the multiplicity of occupational categories the *Handbook*, if perhaps inadvertently, yields a reasonably accurate mapping of lines of economic inequalities with respect to occupation. In other words, if understood as simply a kind of map representing the labor market at a given moment, the *Handbook* might easily seem a rather depressing picture.

Given the position of the job seeker relative to the *Handbook*, however, such a directly centralized affect never becomes an issue. It is possible to imagine without too much trouble, for example, a job seeker agonizingly poised over that piece of information about the frequency of correctional officers who "leave the labor force," wondering whether they left on their feet or on their backs. The way it is presented in the actual *Handbook* text does not exactly encourage such attention. Nor, for that matter, is it discouraged. Surrounded by editorial exhortations regarding how to go about looking for employment, the body of representation in the *Handbook* remains outside any given search, obeying only its own internal logic of relational risks and rewards. The civilian publisher got its start in the 1980s with a book about how to get a job, and it markets the *Handbook* and its various versions thereof around the idea of job hunting. The *Handbook*, however, can saturate so many different forms of job and job-hunting information precisely because it avoids the kind of direct representation that turns up so frequently elsewhere, including that inaugural 1986 publication, appropriately titled *Getting the Job You Really Want*.

In larger terms, it is possible to recognize with respect to some already determinate goal of employment imposed on the *Handbook* from the outside how the notation of limits and barriers functions categorically in any given instance. In each occupational listing the text obligingly identifies the specific requirements that must be mastered to reach the goal. If you choose that occupational category, these are the barriers you must encounter. With respect to the temporality of motion across the *Handbook*'s occupational categories, however, that notation becomes simply a relay switch to the next occupational category. That is, the notation here cycles immediately against the notation there, and so on across the grid. So, far from impeding motion, the notation of limits and barriers accelerates it insofar as any specific notation always requires still another relational measure at another category. The *Handbook* is not a camcorder, but, as Deleuze and Guattari could argue from *1000 Plateaus*, it does a good job of being a textual machine for acceleration.

Thus, although it would be manifestly unfair to claim that the *Handbook* paints a rosy picture of unlimited access to rewarding employment, nevertheless it sets up a powerful countercurrent to the very process of seeking employment that ostensibly functions as the reason for its textual existence at all. The representation that is directly available from the *Handbook* shatters the implied teleology of seeking employment. At least within the temporal duration while the *Handbook* is of use, there is nothing but motion governed by those internal and relational indexes of risk and reward. And if it is possible to imagine a job seeker hung up on any given bit of information, it should be at least plausible as well to imagine being caught up within the *durée* of motion itself.

Here, after all, is a fabulous time of unencumbered virtuality, against which must be measured not only the grim necessity of teleologically determined planning across the hurdles toward a specific employment goal, but also the henceforth ordinary consumer time spent more or less randomly assessing the desirability of this or that consumer good or service or entertainment. For if in one register, as I suggested, it is possible to range the *Handbook* alongside guides to mutual-fund investment similarly foregrounding a calculus of risk and reward, it is no less appropriate to think in terms of something like the on-screen guide to digital cable programming or the shuffle capacity of the iPod. Yet while that fabulous temporality of accelerated motion can be found in these terms as well, the stakes are perhaps not quite equally enticing as in representations of shopping for work. Neither risk nor reward appears with anything like the same significance or charged intensity.

As lived experience, such a virtual temporality of endless motion can be distanced critically, understood as if little more than a form of false consciousness. It is not as though one could avoid forever some fateful telic plunge through the approaching squall line stirred up by the mountain barriers surrounding any given occupational slot. Yet, that distancing also profoundly misreads the diagnostic scan available from guides like the *Handbook* on the very notion of "job" and especially "career." For once entered into the occupational grid mapped in the *Handbook*'s logic of risk and reward, the very idea of a career takes flight beyond the Hollywood-like promise, "He became a certified public accountant and lived happily ever after." The intensities manifested by the *Handbook* are everywhere dependent on the conjunction of time and motion, the *durée* of the virtual search and the ceaseless mobility it makes available. Against such promise, endings—even Hollywood ones—can seem little more than occasional random contingencies to be suffered until a return becomes possible. In any case, given their now widespread availability, texts like the *Handbook* seem almost to invite such inquiry into what is likely to be a very wide-ranging multiplicity of possible responses among individuals. Yet regardless of how it might appear to individuals, within the conditions of a structured program of vocational training and preparation the *Handbook* can also function as a convenient register of shifting internal pressures relative to the labor market that awaits students on completion of their programs.

In a process of cooling out student expectations, information about the labor market typically was tailored to emphasize the difficulty of entry into lucrative and socially prestigious careers. That is, the flow of information moved unidirectionally, toward the end of marking economic fault lines to which students had inevitably to adjust their expectations. As I suggested earlier, the *Handbook* text might continue to be read in these terms, where the sheer exhaustiveness of the data yields a kind of map of the occupational structure of the social formation with its widely differential rewards for specific careers. In the circumstances of reform initiatives that increasingly generate a rhetoric of heating up expectations, however, it is possible to recognize an emergent conception of the labor market that more closely resembles the kind of *internal* logic I have described as governing the *Handbook*'s representation. In this context, even the teleology of Tech Prep, with its carefully sequenced itineraries of preparation, might be understood as little more than a slowing down of the accelerated motion of that internal logic. Like a kind of differential gearbox, Tech Prep planning stages engage available categories of occupation with a plotting of career direction predicated on a potential for improving future outlook over a long-term time. Thus speculation about employment opportunities can continue to take a quite traditional form, in effect betting on a future rise in value relative to any chosen category of occupation. Tech Prep, in other words, preserves a certain long-term perspective on the labor market while at the same time delivering a rationale for heating up rather than cooling out student expectations.

In contrast, proposals for educational preparation such as William Blank's, which I described in chapter 3, lend themselves far more directly to the promise of mobility figured in the *Handbook* imagery of motion across occupational categories. Once having mastered the process Blank identifies as learning how to learn, the student can then put his or her resources at risk in the market, gambling over and over on the quick ability "to acquire the technical aspects" of any job whenever the occasion becomes available. Thus rather than slowing down the immediate conjunction of time and motion in the *Handbook*'s organizing logic, a vision like Blank's would seem to offer instead a means for translating that internal logic directly into perceptions of the labor market. Educational preparation is about equipping the student to play. Once through the barrier of how to learn, the student is then in a position to read the labor market itself in a way more or less congruent with the representation available from the *Handbook*. There is a premium everywhere on calculating the relation of risk and reward, while nevertheless one is also always caught up in a temporality of continual motion, as Blank emphasizes, across occupational category lines that immediately dissolve into the next category.

Risk is built into the *Handbook*'s assessment, but the recognition of a barrier of "how to learn" within the process of educational preparation carries a larger threat of risk. That is, beyond the purely relational indexes that function to accelerate motion through the *Handbook*'s swirl of categories and data "how to learn" appears as an intrusion from outside. It is like a piece of necessary equipment you have to carry into the labor market—or into its textual representation as the *Handbook*—and hence it poses as well a risk that is different in kind. While the rewards for successful passage through the barrier of how to learn are potentially great indeed, the barrier itself marks the threat of a permanent exclusion. It marks something like the return of Grubb's paradox. On one hand, the barrier persists such that one cannot not take the risk of passing without having to face impossibly "dismal" consequences indeed. On the other hand, the risk seems excessive, going far beyond the shifting networks of risk and reward represented in a text like the *Handbook*. Thus, so long as such an educational barrier remains as a limit, there remains also some seemingly irreducible outside to the process of educational preparation where economic inequalities mind their force. That is the prospect, precisely, of permanent exclusion.

In this context the revised testing practices I discussed in chapter 2 assume a special significance. The idea of performance testing as Marc Tucker, for example, elaborates it redistributes the risk of permanent educational failure into something much more closely resembling the relational risk at stake in the *Handbook* indexes. For Tucker, performative success for everyone is contingent on the repeatability of performance. There is always another occasion, and performance can always be repeated differently. Risk is then effectively reassigned to the motor force of repetition. One does not risk the potential permanence of failure across something like the hierarchy of intelligence testing, but simply the continual necessity of creative engagement with the conditions of performance on any given instance. In this sense, risk is impossible to quantify with anything like the static finality of merit determinations. Stakes will reemerge somewhere else; performances can be repeated. More significantly for Tucker, testing thus begins to blur the line between school and work rather than to reinforce a division between an educational process of assessment and actual workplace practices. After all, just as in performance testing, the genuinely creative response to what might otherwise seem an intractable dilemma marks nothing so much as the ultimate motor force of any productive workplace.

The performative risk of testing is offered as a simulation of actual working conditions. In more charged terms, however, that risk becomes nothing less than an immediate and tangible emblem of participation in the far larger, ongoing momentum of the whole vast global economic system. "Capitalism," Ronald Glassman tells us, from the midst of his ostensibly sober sociological scan of a newly emergent class structure in the current economy, "will be an integral part of the high-technology economy of the future, because capitalism motivates productivity, creativity and efficiency" (1997, 23). Capitalism, like Volkswagen, wants drivers, with an educational system that prepares students to risk a new road over and over again in their performances. This is then the point where the shift I have been tracing from a cooling out to a heating up of student expectations reaches an almost eschatological pitch: you are already a winner because you stand at the center of a winning system whose whole reason for being is *your* winning productivity, creativity, and efficiency. At the same time, such an extreme of justification also affords a glimpse into the mechanisms of a larger social process at work in current circumstances.

While the representational power of the *Handbook*'s mapping of an existent labor market with its boundaries and exclusions seems almost to disappear from view, it must be remembered that what lies immediately outside the *Handbook* is less the vast field of the labor market than, precisely, the *search* for employment. Thus the valorization of performative risk as a governing logic of educational preparation offers the means by which something like the *Handbook*'s organization of occupational categories and data can be made to internalize its own previously unrepresentable outside within the terms of educational preparation. What appears in the *Handbook* as the relay switching of notational "limits" and "barriers" re-emerges in the much larger machinery of repetitive performance as both the sign and the instantiation of success, over and over again. No motive appears to arrest the flow, to determine a stable zero sum against which one might measure the relative rate of success and failure, winners and losers. As with viewers of Hollywood's against-all-odds films, "everyone" is already a winner because there is only the search. And nobody ever really loses at shopping.

As vocational-training reforms continue to transform a kind of *Handbook* organizational logic into the conditions of educational preparation, the process of consuming work becomes more and more crucial to the linkage of school and work. Workplace practices no less than school preparation supply the occasion for shopping in effect, for continuing a search for work in the very midst of ongoing school/work activities. Likewise, both everyday "school" and "work" behaviors come to yield the familiar picture of that complex of satisfactions and dissatisfactions associated with a process of consumption. Finally, within these terms of consumption each moment can be charged with the intensity of a futures market that also and simultaneously holds forth the potential of an already financialized asset for continuing the motions of consumption somewhere else.

Yet it is not as if work somehow simply passes from a sphere of production to a sphere of consumption, any more than material, economic inequalities thereby magically disappear from the labor market. Far from it. Any look virtually anywhere (including the *Handbook* itself when read as a map of inequalities) will reveal not only incremental differences in pay scales but also those disturbing gaps where "the same" in terms of available measures of skill and effort nevertheless looks "different" in terms of economic reward. In the midst of what still seemed the booming new economy of the 1990s, Grubb was already arguing that the labor market continued to mark familiar divisions of labor organization. If anything, those divisions seemed to him reified rather than eliminated. The first few years of the twenty-first century both reinforce and extend Grubb's perception. In this sense, nothing seems changed at all—worse, if anything. I argued earlier that "work" brings with it what I called a displaced temporality of necessity, a "dismal" reminder of a kind of dead time of daily, habitual practices whose often meager payoff is always elsewhere. It should now be possible to recognize, however, that the ultimate source of that dead time does not really lie in some ineluctable necessity mysteriously imposed from the outside. Its source is the structural identity between labor organized through exploitative relations to meet the ends of capital, and the social determination and enforcement of economic inequalities.

Nothing has changed—except the *temporal* modality of inequality. Economic inequalities are made to appear as if outside of time, contingent on some impossible Archimedean point outside the flow, an abstract freeze-framing of a dynamic whose reality lies in the endless conjunction of motion and time in the process of consuming work. As dependent on this always mobile temporal modality of inequality, the process of consuming work can effectively dissolve the framing conditions of structural identity between labor organization for capital and social determinations of inequality, without necessarily altering in the least the material conditions of labor. On one hand, the inequalities produced by the organization of labor can be socially consumed under the sign of a radical temporality of motion rather than coalesced into a visibly static divisional hierarchy. Hierarchies impose an iron necessity on the world of work, the visible recognition of steps and barriers in place where one can move only in the prescribed path until reaching her or his individual terminus. In contrast, once in motion inequalities may still stretch as far as the eye can see. But like mall or Main Street, everything becomes a moving, changeable line of stores where one can always hit the next even before dreaming about the one after in the dressing room. With the *Handbook* and the like in hand and onscreen, mapping risk and reward. On the other hand, while stores/categories and shopper/workers move constantly, nothing materially changes about the conditions of labor organization to end or even reduce inequalities. Not because the hidden "reality" remains the same beneath a shifting "appearance," but because the reality of the shifts can always be made to seem infinitely available in one's own favor as you consume inequalities. You're *already* a winner.

Even relatively static hierarchies and steps of labor organization require a process of cooling out student expectations. Along with a number of other processes, ideologies of merit have had a powerful role in that cooling out by helping to reduce the possibility that students would feel the process was unfair. Merit determinations have also played a crucial role in the long and invidious history of blame-the-victim ideologies in the United States. Because they mark relative failure to be the result of inherent individual limitations rather than structural hierarchies already built into the system, they support a claim that victims are not really victims of anything beyond themselves. Rather than a cooling out of expectations, however, work as consumption requires a continual intensification and a vocational training increasingly structured to deliver on the means for heating and reheating expectations at every turn. Together with the temporal flux of inequalities, the heating up helps make the continual preventive maintenance of blame-the-victim ideologies unnecessary. There seems nothing standing still for blame, nothing that victimizes, no reason to look for victims in the first place. Thus, during the 1990s familiar educational policies such as affirmative action began to be represented as simply obsolete rather than wrong because predicated on a rapidly receding structure of external limitations imposed on individuals.

Yet in another sense, and for the same reasons, it is not difficult at all to recognize that the intensity of any individually lived experience of unequal economic relations of employment might well become almost intolerable. Insofar as the temporal horizon of such an experience appears only in dissolve, it no longer seems possible to mobilize one's resources against some massive and static barrier that compels sustained struggle, or even just to subside into passive acquiescence. And where neither struggle nor acquiescence is possible, the experience becomes one of unrelieved turbulence, at worst the intensification of an already intolerable experience. Liberal critics in the 1990s, like Strobel and Peterson, recognized the pervasiveness of economically imposed experiences in these terms as one of the reasons for class polarization. As I pointed out in chapter 2, they saw the explosive combination of individual resentment and widening social disjunction between the few who have benefited immensely from the current economic state and the many increasingly condemned to an underclass as having the potential to ignite class war between haves and have-nots.

Although arguably its sketchiness in Marx permits a great many plausible interpretations, a Marxian theory of class, however, is not necessarily identical with an aggregate charting of individual economic inequalities. Nor is inequality in itself by any means a necessary cornerstone of understanding class social processes. Rather, it is an understanding of class processes that makes it possible to recognize how both the production and consumption of inequalities function in any given configuration of conditions. Consuming work with its correlative heating up of vocational expectations times out the socially programmed inequality connection that had been served by vocational education in the past. But in so doing, it may well also make fundamental class processes and the extent of exploitation visible in very different terms, through the figure of class struggles rather than the specter of underclass resentment that so worries Strobel and Peterson.

CHAPTER 5

Class Processes 101: The Purpose of Competition

A letter to the editor appearing in the *Sacramento Bee* of May 16, 2002, from Curt Augustine, the executive vice president for the California Coalition for Construction in the Classroom, suggests that a college-degree-for-all mentality remains very much the norm, contrary to what William Blank and a great many other reformers had anticipated during the 1980s and 1990s. "I read with dismay," Augustine writes, "but not surprise, of the closure of Sacramento City College's welding program," a closing announced in a *Bee* story dated May 3. His letter continues,

> This is one more unfortunate example of how many of today's educators disregard the needs of students and businesses. At a time when contractors cannot find qualified welders and are forced to bring in out-of-state and foreign welders to finish projects, our schools should be opening more programs. These closings are not solely in community colleges. Since 1982, 60 percent of high school technical education programs in California have closed.... According to the state Employment Development Department, the construction industry has the need for 16,000 new workers a year, yet contractors cannot find enough trained workers today.

Financial support goes to colleges and universities for academic programs, and everyone is encouraged to attend college and get a degree even when his or her prospects may be minimal in contrast to how "industry education programs lead students to high-paying jobs and unlimited opportunities." Augustine lays much of the blame on educators for the decline of training programs. Eager to reproduce their own academic environment, they refuse to acknowledge the completely different needs of business and indeed of students, many of whom would be better served by vocational training for careers in industry trades.

Augustine's complaints have been echoed many times since the 1990s. Nevertheless, his narrow sense of blame and his contempt directed at "foreigners" make it easy to overlook a crucial point about the wider and wider area occupied by an academic environment. This is not only a matter of the pervasiveness of college expectations among students and their parents or the media mantra of "get a degree," but it also becomes an issue of expanding and controlling physical space. The circumstances of the California housing market have been the immediate occasion for many administrators within the University of California system to consider initiatives for supplying or extending some form of university subsidized housing to the huge number of employees required to keep a large state university system running efficiently. Without such available housing, the argument runs, staff members cannot possibly afford to live within even remote commuting distance from the campuses where they work. Nor is the problem confined to staffing. At campuses such as Berkeley, Santa Cruz, and UCLA, beginning faculty also face severe housing dilemmas only partially resolved by programs such as guaranteed mortgage funding and faculty housing. These specifically California concerns reflect part of an increasingly familiar story. Relatively low-paid workers supplying a whole range of in-person services very often must live in remote circumstances from their location of work.

At the same time, more and more colleges and universities market themselves as extraordinarily attractive places to live and work. In *Academic Capitalism and the New Economy*, Sheila Slaughter and Gary Rhoades quote Ernest Boyer's amusing response to promotional literature in *The Undergraduate Experience in America*: "'if we judged from the pictures, it would be very easy to conclude that about half of all college classes in America are held outside, on a sunny day, by a tree, often close to water'" (2004, 287). Later, however, they point to the pervasiveness in the new century of marketing the total physical package of the university: "Colleges and universities are coming to be marketed more as attractive places in which to live, consume services, and play than as challenging places in which to learn and become educated. Ironically, public policy increasingly emphasizes the workforce and economic development roles of higher education, yet in their recruitment efforts institutions are increasingly addressing students' desires as consumers of various consumption item services, as if colleges were a combination of private-sector enterprises and services such as hotels/resorts, restaurants, boutiques, and exercise/fitness facilities" (2004, 298).

Students are not the only ones sold in these terms. Retirement living centers around campuses in university towns have become a major business, often developed in close conjunction with the college or university administration and emphasizing the delights of returning to live near university cultural and sports activities.

These developments emphasize all the more why large universities must employ a great many workers for all kinds of purposes. Indeed, like the immense manufacturing plants of the "industrial past," they are sites of a significant massing of workers at a single location, and like the factory they organize the space to their requirements. The university/factory analogy has been around for a long time, but the emphasis typically has fallen on the degradation of degrees, and students, to the status of an industrial product. The bite of the analogy was assumed to lie in making visible the dangers to valuable educational goals of unrestrained university growth and the subsequent standardization of learning. In contemporary circumstances, however, it seems to me worth refocusing that analogy around what now appears in the United States as the anomaly of such a large workforce concentrated at a single location, with the projection of a corresponding "factory town" enclave of housing surrounding the work location. In other words, the university becomes like a factory less because it mass-produces thousands of degree-widgets than because it can continue to exist in its present form only to the extent that the surrounding environment is transformed into a complex network of job-specific living arrangements. Given the new prominence of online universities and the stagnating promise of far-flung and ostensibly high-tech new educational delivery systems from more "traditional" universities, the UC system seems more and more likely to emerge as a connected series of such university factory towns.

In these terms, the analogy condenses a frequently told tale. The heavy manufacture of durable goods gradually gives way to the production of knowledge and the exchange of information; the routinized assembly-line factory work of the past to the smart work of the present with its premium on innovation and individual responsibility; the factory-central core of production and management to the network of globalized university research connections. Correspondingly, in physical terms the image of the factory town with its rings of drab, massed, uniform housing around the manufacturing plant must give way to the university town image of highly individualized enclaves spreading out from a carefully manicured campus landscape, and often, still farther out, high amenity "villages" reproducing these conditions. As Slaughter and Rhoades put it, what is being marketed to students (and often to retirees) are "attractive places in which to live, consume services, and play" (2004, 298). Politically, the striated antagonism of labor divisions mutates into the interest politics of specific worker aggregates, while meanwhile "town" and "gown" stand in for the stasis of a relatively stable population committed to the area and its "unique character" on one hand and the dynamics of growth through an always larger and transient population of students on the other.

Traditionally, however, higher education has been imagined in the United States as a realm beyond class conflicts where individuals could succeed to the limits of their abilities regardless of background. The symbolic promise of that image suggests still another way of narrating these transitional passages from industrial to postindustrial. As the material embodiment of the ideal of a productive community united around a single collective purpose, the factory town nevertheless was eventually torn apart by the grinding historical force of polarized class interests. Out of the rubble of that failure, the university town then emerges as the symbolic bearer of a reborn unity, the home of an homogeneously productive middle class whose "middleness" remains miraculously unmarked on either side by top or bottom, thereby triumphantly escaping the grimly oppressive history of class conflict that had destroyed the ideal of the factory town. The political payoff for the narrative of passage from industrial to postindustrial production, from factory labor to smart work, is the rebirth of the ideal of an inclusively middle-class workforce whose symbolic home becomes the university town of the future.

It is easy to emphasize the obvious: that actually existent university towns are marked by material distinctions and hierarchies every bit as surely as the factory town of the past, if perhaps in different ways, and more often than not stand in dramatic contrast to adjacent neighborhoods or towns. The discrepancy between symbol and reality is undeniable. Nevertheless, a focus on the sociology of the town (or the campus enclave in a larger urban setting) risks an inability to recognize shifting indexes of class divisions and how they function. Rather than assume that an existent structuring of living arrangements, for example, can immediately translate into the boundary conditions of normative class positions, I think it worth exploring further the larger transformations of labor produced in colleges and universities and valorized under the heading of smart work. Instead of an empty symbolic promise disguising a familiar reality, the university town in these terms appears as a kind of visible metonymy for how class processes are mobilized in ways that do not necessarily depend upon maintaining in disguised form a relatively stable hierarchy of class relations between large groups of the population. That is, the importance of the university town or enclave is less the way it models a changing class structure in itself, whether as symbolic or as material reality, than in how the complex of organized labor functions within the division of class processes. The key to the processes of change on which I will focus is the intensification of competition. Competitive conditions have become so pervasive throughout institutions of higher education that simultaneously they have become almost unnoticeable.

Individualism and the value of competition are such deeply engrained ideologies in the United States in so many different ways that it is tempting to see this intensification as simply pushing competitive pressures a little farther, and tempting as well to see a familiar individualism become a kind of hyperindividualism. As I argued in chapter 2, liberal critics of Reaganism saw the effects of his regime in exactly that way. Economically, competition ran rampant, at the expense of sound, productive investment. Likewise, individualism became so extreme that the social responsibilities of the state to citizens were eroded away.

Rather than simply push the concept to its limit, competition in current circumstances does not fit at all with familiar descriptions. The hyperindividualism of "the winner" must be understood in some other way than as an extension of the individualism of competition. The visibility of hyperindividualist agency, the isolated prominence of "the winner," requires for background what is made to appear as if the by-product or waste of competition as an undifferentiated population mass. By focusing instead on that "waste labor," I want to show how hyperindividualism has emerged as a dominant *class* process built on the subordination of accumulated labor time, and often very skilled work practices, within the waste of competition. Competition intensifies within the educational system where labor time accumulates most directly and where competition can most easily be naturalized.

Despite Curt Augustine's claims, echoed by many others in similar positions, I think it difficult to account for the continuing decline of traditional vocational-training programs on the grounds that educators have channeled students instead toward high-tech, professional, and finance-driven occupations. Doubtless some version or another of Grubb's paradox, discussed in chapter 3, weighs heavily with counselors and instructors. Nevertheless, vocational programs had been declining for some time, and they continued to decline through recent events such as the collapse of the dot-com bubble, the revelation of corporate financial scandals, and the dramatic fluctuations of the stock market. In keeping with the assumption of flexibly general skills applicable to multiple job situations, the process of heating up expectations has not resulted in some clear hierarchy of delimited occupational slots. It is probably true enough, as Augustine's argument implies, that today's high-school students are seldom encouraged by teachers and counselors to think first in terms of training programs for trades such as construction welding. But construction welding and the like are not dismissed in favor of equally occupation specific alternatives. In Kenneth Gray and Edwin Herr's statistics from *Other Ways to Win*, quoted in chapter 3, trades make up a miniscule percentage of jobs that high-school graduates expect to perform. But the preferred alternative of "professional" employment remains obligingly unspecific. The immediate effects of a larger process of heating up expectations appear most visibly only in the kind of negative trajectory that Augustine outlines, as certain opportunities seem to disappear from the horizon.

Regardless, it should be clear that competitive pressures for educational certification and achievement have intensified. As social expectations rise, in whatever indefinite terms, competition heats up as well. In my experience, however, student complaints are couched in terms of the pervasiveness of competition rather than worry that other competitors might be better in specific circumstances. As one student remarked to me after class, "It's like there's nowhere you can go around here without everybody competing over everything." I think that perception enormously important, because the idea of a fair competition assumes specific boundary conditions rather than appearing everywhere all the time. Temporal compressions are important to these particular intensities of competition, but the spatial metaphor is initially useful.

To follow the familiar cliché, it is impossible to "level the playing field" without first assuming a distinct field of competition bounded off from surrounding territory and functioning for the purposes of competition as entirely separate from whatever diverse hilly sectors have produced the competitors. Fairness conflicts have often become almost intolerably frustrating because the intensification of competition affects the determination of boundary conditions and not simply the rules establishing fairness.

That is, it is not just that competition has become so intense that fairness is jeopardized by competitors and others willing to break the rules to win, but also that the very idea of fairness requires a field that is clearly distinct from other fields, and intensification displaces the boundaries that establish distinctness. The result is that any given competitive territory seems immediately open to other territories, where the outcomes of any competition are then affected by considerably more than what happens on a specifically determined "playing field," level or not.

Entrepreneurial competition is the key feature of academic capitalism for Slaughter and Rhoades, but in their 2004 *Academic Capitalism and the New Economy* they recognize that conditions seem to have changed even in relation to Slaughter and Larry Leslie's *Academic Capitalism* in 1997, with its emphasis on the "encroachment" of profit-centered practices into university organization as if the latter were an entirely separate territory. In *Academic Capitalism and the New Economy*, in contrast, the authors stress the methodological difference from other studies of higher education in their approach to issues of boundaries and competition: "In contrast to literatures that focus on 'the' organization or on research relations between universities and industry, construed as separate organizational spheres, we look at networks of actors that cross boundaries among universities and colleges, business and nonprofit organizations, and state(s)" (2004, 9). Their focus is on complex networks of relations among research universities, corporations, and the state, but similar effects of intensified competition appear in everyday college and university situations as well. The perception of grade inflation, for example, suggests that something must have gone wrong with the standards and rules of competition such that far too many students get grades that are far too high. But with the erosion of field boundaries from intensified competition, what appears at the micro level of any specific classroom or even educational institution as an inflated grading process looks on a macro level like an *extension* of a competitive grading process that includes more, and increasingly more diverse, sectors of the social formation generally. Grading, like everything else, seems caught in always expanding networks of relation.

The apparent contradiction of grade inflation occurring simultaneously with intensified competition can be resolved in part by a recognition of this extension of a process of grading to include an always widening range of educational and workplace networks of relations. Grade inflation is perhaps better understood as the inflation of grading to cover more and more social territories. It may well be true enough that a much larger percentage of students at a particular high school are perceived as having inflated GPAs that meet college admission standards. But that is hardly the end of the story. Relatively few nevertheless will actually be admitted to the college "of their choice." The high-school grade inflation that yields such a high percentage of potential college admissions is subjected to an expanded grading scale that ranks different colleges and universities and distinguishes among those potential admissions. Farther down the line, the 3.6 GPA that might well have signaled admission into a graduate school from the undergraduate level turns into a mark of failure as a graduate-school grade. Likewise, at the graduate level, departmental admissions committees not only weigh differently a 3.6 GPA and a 3.8 GPA from the same undergraduate institution, but also weigh differently a 3.8 GPA from Institution One and a 3.8 GPA from Institution Two. Students in turn evaluate different schools not only in relation to internal grading norms and success rates, but also and more significantly to job-placement statistics. Quite rightly, students must worry not only about how well they do in relation to other students in their schools, but also about how well their particular institution stacks up with other institutions, and so on through more and more complexities of distinction across more and more sectors. As Slaughter and Rhoades suggest, existing networks of social relations embed actors in multiple territories simultaneously.

Like Slaughter and Rhoades, however, I have also slipped into a language of boundary erosion in describing conditions of intensified competition, as if field markers are gradually wearing down in ways that then allow more and more spillage from one field to the next. Rather than erosion or permeability, I want to suggest it might be more accurate to understand competition intensifying as time speeds up, accelerating the flow of effects across multiple territories. The sustained long moment of competitive encounters valorized in classical conceptions of competition seems no longer available, no isolated duration possible. It is as if at any given moment one is already forced to inhabit a future dragging along the results of the previous encounter while simultaneously trying to glimpse what seems to be happening two or three alongside and ahead. Thus the result is less like the slow, steady erosion of formerly stable boundaries than multiple series of rapid lightning flashes, suddenly illuminating far too much for far too short a time. "It's like there's nowhere you can go around here without everybody competing over everything," and at every flash there's more to see beyond any existent walls, regardless of whether eroded or still intact.

Classical conceptions of competition always include some idea of a neutral and arbitrating position where the only stake is to ensure the competition has been carried out as it should be. Sometimes a blind or invisible force occupies that position—"the invisible hand," for example, so beloved by neoclassical economists as governing the market. Sometimes, most obviously in sports, it is occupied by specific individuals who as referees or umpires are responsible to the organization of the sport itself as existing outside any given game-day competition. Intensified competition, however, not only threatens field boundaries, but in so doing also jeopardizes the authority of the position responsible for the integrity of the competition. If every territory can be affected by others beyond it, then no guarantees exist for the neutrality or independence of any possible adjudicating agency. As those who watch sports scoring (or presidential elections) see over and over, every position seems potentially at stake rather than securely outside the action. Correlatively and perhaps even more significant, it becomes increasingly difficult to isolate the integrity of the individual competitive unit, let alone the referee.

A student might well be tempted to cheat on exams, for example, in hopes of gaining a competitive advantage over other students. But what is available to one student is likely available to others who inhabit other territories as well. When more and more students begin to cheat in multiple ways, what happens is not really an automatic edge of any one student over other students, but rather the blurring of boundaries that differentiate one student as individual from another individual. Likewise, in sports competitions "bodies" begin to blur in something of the same way as "minds" in scholastic competitions. Body A on steroids becomes increasingly indistinguishable from sports body B on steroids. Drug use in sports, like cheating on exams, appears a violation of the individual "unit" of competition, but in larger terms what has happened is a kind of expanded grading scale that now incorporates formerly external factors internally into the game's competitors. Which drugs you use can make a great deal of performance difference. Economically, something very similar happens to the supposedly individual corporate entity in competition with similar entities. The routinely misnamed operation of a corporate buyout or takeover might better be understood within this new order of competition as instead a response, precisely, to an inflation of grading scale such that formerly distinct corporate boundary terms can no longer usefully identify the competitive stakes.

Bodies blur, minds strategize indistinguishably, but at the same time competitive stakes are as important as ever. In recent discussions of a putatively sudden increase of steroid use in baseball, for example, players are frequently quoted as claiming in effect that steroids will turn a mediocre athlete into major-league quality, a superior athlete into a superstar, and a superstar into legend material—not simply that steroids blur all athletes into the same *status*. Individual bodies may blur, but the categories denoting relative status seem to remain intact. Educator alarm over grade inflation may project a dismal classroom filled with individual mediocrities listing 3.8 GPAs and going on to graduate. But during the period from 1985 to 1995, when presumably the dual process of lowered standards and grade inflation would have been accelerating exponentially, the percentage of high school graduates who actually *finished* a college degree ten years out from high school barely rose at all. As vocational-training reformers often point out, it remained just under 25 percent, despite the fact that the percentage of those who report some college coursework has been rising dramatically. Very recent statistics indicate that percentage has only risen to slightly over 27 percent for *everyone* over twenty-five who graduated from high school. The inflation of grading seems to continue producing winners and losers, even though intensified competition significantly alters familiar ways of understanding competitive processes.

In these circumstances, however, "winning and losing" seems more appropriate than "winners and losers," with its suggestion of distinct individual competitors. Winning becomes positional in relation to a scale of effects rather than as an indexical order of individual competitors that yields a "winner." Familiarly the position of winner exists only in relation to the others in a determined field of competition, each competitor precisely placed relative to the others by the finish. The inflation of grading shifts the determination of winning position from this hierarchical freeze frame to what seems the potentially endless rippling out of effects across the multiple sectors brought into play by the extensions that come with the inflation of grading. To modify the Olympic Games truism, it is not just that no one remembers the silver-medal winner, but also that few will remember for long *which sport* produced which silver medal. For the "gold" is measured less in terms of the other competitors in a given sport than in terms of all the effects it sets in motion, from TV guest appearances to Wheaties boxes and endorsements everywhere.

What remains of a traditional idea of competition and its winner is only a kind of retrofit of "the gold position" to a psychological imaginary of the individual. The individual competitor can be extravagantly lauded as a hero because the circumstances of competition no longer involve individual units at all. Hence the inevitable sports retrospective, for example, where endless analysis is devoted to identifying those special qualities of the individual winner that already guaranteed an outcome only visible finally at the end of the competitive struggle. As in that current form of the against-all-odds film plot mentioned many times before, "winning" in this imaginary only confirms what must already have been the case. Winning then seems available to anyone who competes with real intensity—you are already The One.

But only in retrospect. The familiar individual-writ-large of celebrity culture becomes one obvious result, as if a steroid boost to one of the most deeply ingrained U.S. ideologies and confirmed by the proliferating retrospect of daily celebrity behavior offered in *People, US Weekly, Star*, and so on through by now a huge list. A whole range of effects is made to appear coextensive with an already isolated and discrete individual's power of agency acting on his or her circumstances.

If inadvertently, Michael Barone's *Hard America, Soft America* (2004) can help explain how that retrofit imaginary works. Although his text looks rather like a spam porn ad, with its capital letters "H" and "S" throughout, Barone's basic idea seems to be that everything valued by softie coddlers depends on those *really* hard individuals willing to compete to bring out their best: "Soft America lives off the productivity, creativity, and competence of Hard America, and we have the luxury of keeping parts of our society Soft only if we keep enough of it Hard" (2004, 16). Unlike more traditional descriptions of the individual competitive self, however, where the winning individual appears at the top of an elaborate hierarchy of individual competitors, the phantom individual who plays the hero role in Barone's metacompetition between competition and coddling exists only after the fact, in relation to an anonymous mass. That is, "Hard" equals individuated, standing out in contrast to an amorphous and undifferentiated soft mass—which presumably is why we only need to "keep enough of it Hard" to get the job done. Though doubtless he despises "softie" Hollywood, the picture he presents has a lot more in common with the isolated star surrounded by anonymous adoring fans than with older descriptions of competition among the "real men" Barone wants us all to start adoring again.

Rather than one individual competitor among others, the winner who appears in Barone's description is a kind of projected afterimage of hyperindividualism as a class process. In this psychological retrofit, hyperindividualism may then seem like just an extreme version of familiar individualistic ideologies. But as Barone's commentary inadvertently reveals, the mechanisms at work are very different indeed. The classic "winner" is the best individual, and competition has sorted out the hierarchy of individuals. In contrast, as a class process hyperindividualism requires instead an apparently absolute gap between winner and mass, with no linking hierarchies of sorted out individuals. Focusing on class processes, however, requires a shift of attention away from the direct intensities of the competitive process to what the imaginary of winning position can register only as a kind of buildup of detritus or waste by-product left behind in the wake of the heat of competition. Refocused instead in relation to class processes, this "waste" reemerges as specific forms of exploited labor, the subordination necessary to sustain the dominance of hyperindividualism.

Karl Marx identified a passage from what he called the formal subsumption of labor to capital to a real subsumption where it was no longer necessary to bring into the process forms of labor that had originated outside capitalist production. Commenting on Marx's account, however, Michael Hardt and Antonio Negri argue in *Empire* that his "intuitions of the process of real subsumption do not furnish us with the key we need. The passage from the formal subsumption to the real must be explained through the practices of active subjective forces. . . . In this sense, the processes of the formal subsumption anticipated and carried through to maturity the real subsumption, not because the latter was the product of the former (as Marx himself seemed to believe), but because in the former were constructed conditions of liberation and struggle that only the latter could control" (2000, 255–256). Rather than simply some implacable logic of capital proceeding toward always greater control over labor practices, their argument is that a real subsumption was a reactionary response to the "active subjective forces" of workers that had been possible to set in motion because of the conditions of formal subsumption.

One would not necessarily expect to draw support for Hardt and Negri's arguments from Harry Braverman's analysis in *Labor and Monopoly Capital*, but his discussion of the real subsumption of labor suggests that management control in response to labor activities was indeed a central factor. Braverman is much more closely focused on labor practices than are Hardt and Negri, emphasizing Marx's recognition that real subsumption involved an elaborate reorganization of the labor process itself according to the requirements of capital. Thus, in his discussion of scientific management techniques Braverman points out how at each step the labor processes involved were subjected to a direct intervention of planned programming, atomizing the tasks in production, often recombining them in entirely different ways and introducing new technologies with the result that the labor process no longer operated the same. "Efficiency" was the official rationale developed for scientific management, whether on the assembly line or, as Braverman wonderfully demonstrates, in the organization of office practices, and in Marxian terms efficiency meant the conditions for intensifying exploitation.

Yet Braverman also repeatedly emphasizes how the result was a radical reduction of worker autonomy and a powerful augmentation of management control. With the production process divided into discrete units and each worker responsible for only one unit, it was far less likely that anyone outside of management would have an understanding of the whole process. Access to and control over that knowledge was reserved for management. Correspondingly, shop alliances that had often been based on shared covert knowledge became increasingly more difficult. Efficiency in any case meant the kind of speedup that made routine interactions among workers nearly impossible. Each worker became an isolated unit, an extension of the specific task assigned in production. As Hardt and Negri speculate, the net effect was management's ability to exert far more complete control over the large number of laborers often required by any given production process and to forestall organized worker challenges.

Against the background of this analysis, it may well seem that more recently such control has broken down or deliberately been altered by very different ways of conceiving the role of management. During the 1980s and 1990s there was a significant reaction against top-down management organization, often directed against the kind of control exercised through scientific management and its successors. The figure of the micromanager obsessively looming over his subordinates' work became almost a figure of fun. At the same time, it is not as if the perception of controlling forces disappeared. I pointed earlier to Carl Augustine's letter to the *Sacramento Bee* protesting the closing of the construction-welding program at the city college as an example of misunderstanding the new pressures of heightened social expectations, as if the closure were purely the result of educators insensitive to business needs. But the letter is also an expression of anger at control slipping away, always appearing to be somewhere else. After all, the effect of the school closure will not be to slow down new construction so that Augustine and other employers could end up without a job themselves. The construction trades continue to be in high demand. Augustine is frustrated at the lack of control by employers over not only the potential behaviors of those out of state and foreign welders he deplores having to hire, but also the training and credentialing process for available workers.

Hiring a construction workforce now seems to require a decidedly second-order operation. Augustine and others like him must reactivate what in his eyes appears as an inert and undifferentiated labor pool whose qualifications are at best unknown and at worst suspect as perhaps simply discards from some other work site or even some other field of work altogether. It no longer seems possible to draw directly from a pool of already available skilled labor whose individual qualifications are a matter of record, vouched for by a familiar educational training in terms that make sense for the job. Such control has slipped away, and instead it seems vested in an educational system no longer responsive to the needs of the construction group employers he represents. Educational institutions, though, are not responsible for these circumstances, as Augustine suggests; similar frustrations are expressed in them all the time, even at the most prestigious level of institution. The content is different, but the point is the same as Augustine's: control has not disappeared at all but simply gone somewhere else, slipped out of the "right" hands where it belongs.

The perception of widespread grade inflation, to continue my earlier example, means that graduate admissions committees in a number of disciplines echo Augustine at nearly every meeting. Everybody's grades look great, so the committee must choose from within a large pool of largely undifferentiated candidates who may well all be mediocrities anyway, at least in the eyes of the committee members. Nevertheless, such a committee itself is likely to ignore altogether whatever specific details (GPA and otherwise) that do appear among applicants below a certain cutoff line. That is, the intricacies of distinction at each undergraduate institution attended by those applicants are suddenly and dramatically compressed into a single determination of failure relative to a continuing and highly individualized attention to applicants above whatever has been determined as a cutoff line. Thus given the dramatic increase in temporary, adjunct, and part-time appointments in a number of disciplines, one also often hears expressions of something very like Augustine's frustration at the prospect of picking among discards and failures to fill out a workforce. Likewise, with the intense competitive pressures to admit a student cohort equal to the most prestigious research universities, faculty at slightly less prestigious schools are often bitterly disappointed at losing top candidates and "forced" to make decisions among "also-rans."

A large, undifferentiated pool of available labor sounds a lot like the familiar Marxian concept of a reserve army produced among other things by the real subsumption of labor to capital. The differences, however, are significant. A reserve army was recognized by individual employers as a good thing for them, an aggregate group of nonworkers whose existence supplied a lever to exercise against their current employees. In contrast, employer perceptions of a current pool of undifferentiated labor suggest that it is probably made up of discards and also-rans, basically a waste compared to the more desirable—and unavailable—workers gone elsewhere. Nevertheless, unlike the basically unskilled labor required from a reserve army, waste labor is expected to perform comparatively very skilled labor across quite a wide range of positions, usually in ways that do not differ appreciably from how it might be performed by a more "elite" pool. The daily work of graduate teaching assistants at their second, third, or fourth choices of graduate programs where they were finally admitted does not differ much from the daily practices of those teaching assistants who would have been doing the teaching had they not instead competitively "succeeded" to their first choice of programs and gone elsewhere. For all his complaints, Augustine's "imported" construction welders do basically the same kind of work as his more desirable employees would have done.

Whatever actual skills might have been possessed by individuals who were a part of a reserve army, their labor was in demand as unskilled and basically interchangeable workers. Waste-labor workers instead are indistinguishable only when remaining within the undifferentiated pool perceived as waste labor. Reactivation is also individuation in ways that require often very specific skills across a great many different positions. This contrast between waste labor and a reserve army helps a great deal to explain how the process of management control has changed. In current circumstances, work practices need not be controlled by a direct intervention in and reorganization of the labor process, or on the basis of superior knowledge over the whole process of work in contrast to the discrete areas of knowledge possessed separately by each worker. In other words, the most visible characteristic distinguishing a real subsumption of labor to capital for both Marx and Braverman would no longer function in the same way.

Work practices do not need to be designed and controlled by management because waste labor is already skilled labor. The greatest leverage point of authority exists at the moment of *hiring*, understood in the sense I described above as if a second-order operation reactivating laborers from what appears otherwise to employers as an inert and undifferentiated labor pool. Once hired, however, their work practices have not necessarily been determined by active management control, and what direct control does exist can be exercised sporadically rather than continuously. Assessment in all its multiple forms replaces scientific management, exercising a very different kind of control. To put it more generally again, the subsumption of labor to capital no longer requires a direct interventional reorganization of labor processes. Subsumption instead feeds off the conditions of competition that make available a large, skilled, and, from the point of view of capital, a largely undifferentiated pool of discards or waste labor awaiting reactivation in a second-order entry into an actual labor process.

Whether construction welding, teaching and research within a discipline, or any of a wide range of examples that could be adduced, the labor required by specific tasks is figured across a strikingly divided set of conditions. The labor process seems to possess a certain direct immediacy linked to a performance determined by the parameters of the task and resulting in measurable outcomes in some form or another. Yet it appears as *labor* at all only by virtue of an increasingly complicated network of competitively graded scaling decisions. Those decisions involve individuals, programs, and institutions that must at some point be lumped indiscriminately as failures that will then undergo a second-order reactivation that identifies their participation in the direct immediacy of a given labor process. Were the terms not already long ago reserved to rather different meanings, it would be possible to say that the "concrete labor" engaged in a specific process is through and throughout determined by a calculus of "abstract labor" whose condition of reference is neither labor in the first sense at all, nor the determination of labor power across the specifics of a given production process. Abstract labor in this sense depends on the process of intensified competition driven by the collapsing boundaries of the inflation of grading in all its multiple forms across the social formation.

Understood in these terms, abstract labor thus points toward the larger terms of a fundamental division of class processes. Abstract competitive intensities divide across hyperindividualism as a dominant class process and waste labor as subordinate class processes. Waste labor in turn is fed by a still more subordinate heterogeneous mass whose members must then be solicited everywhere in the culture to stay in school, get an education, get a degree while meanwhile performing the lowest level of jobs—if any. From the point of view of a dominant class, waste labor requires a second-order reactivation to emerge from conditions of competitive failures. In contrast to a direct, top-down control of daily labor practices, however, this second-order process often seems to yield only second-best products, with more powerful authority always vested somewhere else. In response to the perceived vulnerability, hiring and firing become far more common, which in turn accelerates the necessity for continued reactivation of waste labor and more workers fed into waste labor from below. From the other side, however, waste labor appears as subordinate class processes, determined by exploitation as the extraction of surplus labor. The dominance of hyperindividualism makes exploitation at once more complicated and yet, paradoxically, simpler and more directly abstract and general as well.

The complications result from the networked layering of competitive exchanges, the inflation of grading in the ways it develops extensively across more and more sectors. Competition at each step and each moment of exchange requires labor toward the end of producing a *general* surplus of skills. From the top, the perspective of individual managers like Augustine, control may then seem precarious because this relatively more complicated process does not necessarily yield either skill or, ultimately, surplus labor to any given individual investor in the process. The "success" of exploitation in these terms depends instead on the abstract generality of competitive intensities as they produce a skilled surplus. At the same time, however, intensified competition also permits a relatively much more direct exploitation of the labor involved insofar as it is no longer necessary to introduce radical changes in the everyday organization of work practices. The difficult reorganization that might have entailed hiring a scientific management consultant to subdivide tasks in production, calculate new efficiency ratios, and so on, can be replaced by the brutally direct process of "downsizing" experienced workers and reactivating the always more available waste by-product of competition. Only in fantasies like Barone's neoconservative spam sitcom does competition simply bring out the best in everyone. It functions in class terms to ensure a continual supply of waste labor for exploitation.

Historically, vocational education had been designed to supply an industrial working class to a rapidly changing economy and population. Although modified in a great many ways over the next few decades, vocational-education programs after World War II continued in something close to that original role by way of the psychological emphasis on cooling out. The shift from cooling out to heating up expectations signals a larger shift in function from the production of an industrial working class to the production of the skilled surplus required by exploitation under the dominance of hyperindividualism as a class process. Correspondingly, waste labor does not require stable hierarchies of the kind that older vocational-education programs had helped to build. It depends instead on renewable competition that can produce an instant hierarchy on any given occasion while simultaneously holding out the promise to the losers that next time you might be the one. Competition has intensified in ways that continually add new territories as competitively available and leap the boundaries that had marked a competitive "playing field."

Waste labor does not depend on permanently stable hierarchies, but that does not mean that hierarchies have collapsed. The factory town virtually disappeared some time ago, and along with other educational programs the training formerly known as vocational education has been invited to live in the suburbs of the university town of the future as it stands in symbolically for the new promise of an endlessly inclusive middle class. The peripheral suburbs, however, still look depressingly similar. Only the price is higher, and they are inhabited already by a Christian right with its own versions of increasingly rigid hierarchy and intense competitiveness. For all that I have emphasized the differences between waste labor and the Marxian concept of a reserve army, in this context there is one overwhelmingly important similarity. Both serve their respective functions initially as a large, undifferentiated mass of workers. The constant heating up of expectations becomes always more necessary, to solicit everyone possible into the mass of waste labor and to play over and over that familiar against-all-odds plot with its terminal explanations of how you are already the one, already and always on your way up. What is below meanwhile becomes more and more invisible, as if nothing exists at all but the top and those who want to be there.

CHAPTER 6

Competition, Choice, and the Management of Class Doubling

Undergraduates at colleges and universities are frequently linked in more and more complicated ways with community-college, distance-educational, and vocational-technical students. Very often the same person is all of the above. Transferring from one institution to another, changing programs and majors, reducing class schedules while working full-time, sitting out for a year and often more, dropping out altogether only to return some years later somewhere else in some entirely different set of circumstances, have all become commonplace. Nevertheless, such increasingly routine behaviors distinguish this large and heterogeneous group from those who never finish high school, who drop out well before they could even begin these mazy itineraries. In California the dropout rates are especially high for African American and Latina/Latino students, and rates have continued to rise over the period since Proposition 13 began the long, steady decline of the California public school system. Like unemployment statistics that make perfect sense so long as people who have no paying jobs are not counted, the idea of no child left behind makes equal sense if you can forget the ones left out altogether.

All this forgetting becomes considerably easier because of how competitive pressures make it seem as if nothing matters anyway except success at the upper reaches of prestigious educational institutions. Thus, dominant class processes now magnify the longstanding idea of "the undergraduate" as defined from a clear top-down perspective. The academic capitalism anatomized by Sheila Slaughter, Larry Leslie, and Gary Rhoades invites a focus on undergraduates as if they were already professionals, potential researchers, and entrepreneurs. Faculty in research universities are continually encouraged to find ways of including more undergraduates in research, often in conditions that in the not too distant past would have applied only to graduate students. High-prestige universities recruit incoming classes with an eye toward garnering a reflected prestige from their accomplishments in specific fields to distinguish the university from direct competitors and from the lower echelons of prestige. Elizabeth Duffy's 1998 book *Crafting a Class* largely focuses on this shift toward admissions policies that look first to potential returns from eventual graduates, in terms of both prestige and money. In *Academic Capitalism and the New Economy*, Slaughter and Rhoades extend Duffy's argument to consider how admissions choices also attempt to establish what amounts to a brand image for the university. It is true enough, as they acknowledge, that not every school is "of a size and selectivity to afford admissions officers the same options in crafting a class that those at highly selective institutions have" (293). Nevertheless, once such institutions establish the practice, it then becomes an end in itself for other institutions as an indicator of prestige.

The continuing-education or distance-education units of colleges and universities cannot quite craft a class or a brand name in these terms. But definitions from the top create opportunities nevertheless to recruit selectively. Programs can take advantage of new educational job requirements in a way that results in a relatively more homogeneous population among the ranks of already employed professionals and upper-level service workers. Slaughter and Rhoades argue that this also means less access for many others: "The knowledge economy calls for white-collar, service workers to repeatedly upgrade their skills to keep pace with changes in the technology-intensive workplace. Increasingly these workers turn to continuing education and distance education. We believe this process expands existing socioeconomic inequalities. The white-collar workers that colleges and universities have targeted as markets are part of an already employed class of professional and managerial workers. Colleges and universities pay less attention to expanding initial access for growing numbers of historically underserved student populations" (285). Initial access is impossible anyway for that large percentage of "historically underserved student populations" who never finish high school. When it is possible, the duration and quality of access become equally important as students move in and out of different educational institutions over longer periods of time.

Even though it seems remote in the midst of the Bush regime, the political imaginary of an all-inclusive middle class that contributed so much to vocational-training reform initiatives in the 1980s and 1990s has not yet disappeared. The competitive intensities of class processes, more than the red/blue values divide, transform visions of inclusiveness into merely some massy indeterminate background against which positions at the top can then be distinguished from the mass. Likewise, definitions from the top of "the undergraduate" function to emphasize competitive success for a few as defining parameters for the undergraduate, and to push into obscurity the network of connections linking college and university undergraduate programs with the immense range of other postsecondary educational programs and institutions. The changes in vocational training over the last few decades suggest good reason instead to think in terms of definitions that understand "undergraduate" less in relation to future researchers and professionals than as a multidimensional population with all the complex connections to postsecondary programs of various kinds that designation implies.

In their worst-case scenario for the future of the entrepreneurial research university in their 1997 *Academic Capitalism*, Slaughter and Leslie anticipated a positioning of undergraduate education as a kind of punishment for those disciplines and faculty members unable to play the academic capitalism game at a high level: "for example, physics departments may teach undergraduates whereas materials sciences centers become heavily involved in academic capitalism. . . . Generally, faculty in fields close to the market will teach less; those far from the market, more. Greater numbers of part-timers will be hired, until teaching departments have small cores of full-time faculty and large contingents of part time faculty, graduate assistants, and technical staff. The full-time faculty far from the market will have little time for research and scholarship" (243). While they did not remark upon it at the time, increasingly this teaching takes place among an undergraduate population likely to be composed of students of different ages who have some combination of college or university courses, community-college courses, vocational-training programs, and on-the-job training, nearly all of whom nevertheless expect outstanding personal success from college. Much teaching of this sort is already being outsourced from research universities. Slaughter and Rhoades comment that "the percentage of faculty who are part-time has doubled in the last twenty years" (332). Teacher labor is cheaper than upper-level research labor, but it becomes cheapest of all when its practitioners are prevented from being in any position to make significant claims for doing research.

What Slaughter and Leslie imagine for physics departments is even more true for disciplines in the humanities where large departments such as English have been outsourcing a good deal of teaching for some time, despite efforts by the Modern Language Association and other national organizations. Nearly every indicator suggests that, in the humanities at least, Slaughter and Leslie's "worst case" may already have arrived. Nevertheless, the definitional power of graduate-school research on the imaginary of "the undergraduate" makes it extremely difficult for conceptions of teaching in the humanities to escape the gravitational pull of research directions in textual scholarship. Despite the fractional percentage of English majors, for example, who eventually go on to graduate school in English, the issues are all too often represented as if a "crisis" that somehow we in the humanities must find a way to resolve. Thus, like many others in these assessing-the-ongoing-crisis modes, David Laurence in his address to the College English Association (CEA) in 2002, "The Latest Forecast: The Future of the English Profession," looks inside for the source of the trouble.

The basic problem as he sees it is that we argue too much among ourselves about our sectarian research interests in a way that leaves little apparent grounds of consensus, especially given the demo job that theory performed on a lot of cherished assumptions. As a result, we have not done a very good job explaining to others exactly what we do. In future we must reach some consensus that allows us to represent ourselves more positively, taking care especially "to describe the educational goods from studies undertaken in our departments in such a way as to make evident how these goods are unmistakably specific to us—to our departments and our subject area. That is, the accounts we formulate should not be pitched at so high a level of generality that they make what we do more or less identical to humanistic or the liberal arts at large. This is one weakness I see in accounts that stake their appeals on terms such as 'critical thinking' or 'reading, writing, and literacy'" (10). As his litany implies, Laurence thinks such things are not only far too general, shared across all the humanities, but also depressingly service-oriented skill training, having little to do with our specific research interests.

While his marketplace language of "educational goods" may strike some as offensive, taking it at face value suggests that at the very least Laurence apparently has forgotten how markets are typically described. It does not really matter what goods we supply or how unique they are if there is no demand for them, and among many other visible signs the proliferation of crisis statements such as his own indicates that there is probably not a massive pent-up demand for textual studies just waiting out there if only we could explain ourselves better. More directly, Laurence's skepticism about the high level of generality required by appeals to "critical thinking" or "reading, writing, and literacy," with the implied risk of becoming indistinguishable from the rest of the humanities, seems singularly misplaced. Literary study would never have existed in anything like its twentieth-century institutionalized forms without that level of generality. In common with the rest of the humanities in one way or another, English always has been in the business of literacy in the broadest sense of that now very multifaceted term. In one way or another, literacy defines the complex commerce through which academic disciplines in the humanities engage with the surrounding social world. It is not as if somewhere in the late 1940s it occurred to a bunch of state legislatures simultaneously that the country would be in grave danger unless scholars at major universities started pumping out tens of thousands of excruciatingly detailed interpretive essays a year on every author who would be included in the *Norton Anthology*. It is only as attached to, and made intelligible by, very general perceptions of literacies and their value that specific and familiar versions of literary study became educationally viable at all.

In her response to Laurence at the CEA forum, Patricia Harkin argued effectively that by assigning basic problems to internal turbulence he manages to ignore far more considerable external factors: "From my perspective, the unhappy situation in which we find ourselves is not the result of single, disparate causes but rather of multiple, overdetermined explanations that are embedded in capitalism and therefore far beyond the control of English departments, even if they were, by some miracle, to decide to act in unison." In one sense she is right. Even closer to home than she implies, it is useless to imagine that the academic capitalism Slaughter and Leslie discuss would go away if we seriously rethought the concept of aesthetics or started doing really, really materialist analysis of texts or invented another and still more specific level of historical detail. Or if, in unison, we found a way-cool rhetoric to explain to everybody what all that was all about. In another sense, however, given that we are in the literacy business, there ought to be ways to understand better how it works in its various versions, where and how multiple humanities departments do business and with whom, and quite possibly how to redirect some of business as usual toward creating better conditions for students—for *undergraduate* students, in terms that recognize how vocational training and class formation have become very much a postsecondary process.

Fortunately, Laurence seems to be speaking for a dwindling minority position. A great many people in English, and certainly in writing programs and in education, do know a great deal about the considerable new bodies of research represented by New Literacy studies, multimodal literacy studies, and historical studies in a number of areas. Obviously it is important to look at the sociocultural contexts that condition how literacy in whatever form is acquired, as does most research in New Literacy studies, or at relations to specific technologies, as in multimodal studies. It seems to me equally important, however, to explore the shifting social values and roles assigned to literacy in all its forms. My argument about the postsecondary location of conditions of class formation and vocational training implies that the advanced-literacies part of that training has been revalued and repositioned significantly. Even more significant for my purposes, academic literacies have become very much a part of work that is governed through management and the exploitation of labor. The skills and skill training involved, as well as the complex ensembles of relation with different technologies, are increasingly defined through the conditions of work and postsecondary locations of vocational training. I am not at all suggesting that the survival of the humanities might depend on some wholesale transformation of textual studies into literacy studies. While it is useful to study specific literacy skills and new forms of literacy, those of us in humanities disciplines are primarily positioned to *manage* literacy work carried out by various groups in postsecondary institutions. Thus, rather than imagine a shift to literacy study as a new focus of research interest, it seems to me necessary first to understand how management processes function.

For some time, the relative academic success of English perhaps even more than other humanities disciplines depended to some very great extent on its credentialing authority, far more than on skill training or even ideological inherence. As different literacy specifics bind with new technologies and social locations, however, the general authority vested in that credentialing process can no longer be relied on implicitly. While the cultural capital associated in the past with disciplinary credentialing wanes, the positioning as academic-literacy managers becomes more pervasive. The shock of that movement has been considerable. Hence the "crisis" that Laurence and so many others refer to so often, which is generally what it feels like when you lose what you could not be bothered to notice in the first place. The issue in any case is not the survival of the humanities, which have never survived long in any specific configuration anyway, but what those of us who teach in humanities disciplines can contribute to changing the conditions of undergraduate education. Those future possibilities depend on understanding how management works, and that understanding can begin by asking what class processes require of academic management in the complex circumstances of postsecondary vocational training.

Ideologically, the central building block of a capitalist wage-labor system was seen as the freedom of workers to sell the labor power they owned. The free sale of labor not only distinguished the wage laborer from the slave but also invested the worker in the process of production. Hyperindividualistic agency, by contrast, invests workers as consumers. Even in the midst of labor, one can always be in search of work. The result contributes to an ideological shift from the freedom of selling one's labor power to the power of choice. The idea of choice stands to the current competitive intensities of capitalism as the idea of freely exchanging one's labor power for a wage did to an earlier capitalism. In one sense, that might seem simply a general extension of an older freedom of choosing to sell one's labor power, ideologically extending the idea of free choice beyond work itself to offer an empowering of individual agency across a wide range of everyday life. In another sense, choice in this register owes less to an older world of production than to the entirely different coordinates of contemporary consumption in its relation to class processes.

As with any form of shopping in a capital-driven consumer marketplace, work as consumption foregrounds agency as choice among seemingly endless possibilities. No one is anywhere working except by choice; no one gets anywhere else except by choice; to be successful you have to choose success, and so on. Freedom means the assurance that choice has not been blocked through some residual set of circumstances that must soon be banished to a permanent past; small wonder that across the spectrum in current U.S. politics so many debates invariably turn on what program/policy/party can be seen to best promote the most meaningful choices. Within media culture, choice appears everywhere. Before being a winner one must choose to win, as featured daily in the endless versions of reality television where the claim to reality is precisely the totalizing pervasiveness of competition involving long sequences of choices. Although there are markets in virtually everything, and although they work in countless different ways, the dominant media *image* of "market" is of course the stock market, where choices seem rapid and dramatic, the effects immediately visible, and the wisdom of choosing correctly at the right time the most prized possession of all. What Jeremy Rifkin and others could refer to in the 1990s as the end of work might be better understood as the insertion of work into the seamless and seemingly endless belts of consumption where choice is everything. As I argue in *Everyday Exchanges* (1998), every area of life can then be directly connected to multiple forms of work and hence ultimately available to exploitation in all the new forms exploitation can now take.

The idea of selling one's labor power functioned among other things to disguise the economic process of exploitation and the realities of work, which then returned in the displaced form of that familiar modern narrative of an individuality lost in the anonymity and alienation of an industrial age. As a now-pervasive construct, however, choice no longer requires similar distinctions between appearance and reality, but rather resolves events into a kind of looping continuum. Because a shift at any crucial nexus of events appears as though always articulated through choices, elaborate distinctions among kinds of events seem unnecessary and disguise irrelevant. Rather than the alternatives of alienation or integration, each successive event simply compounds competitive pressures and intensifies the imaginary of choice. Rather than individuality that must be recovered through the compensatory politics of citizenship equality or the pleasurable distractions of consumption against the alienation of work, dominant hyperindividualism offers both citizenship and consumption as already inherent in competitive labor. "For the first time since the industrial revolution," Lauren Resnick and John Wirt can remind us again in their globalizing introduction to vocational training reform, "the demands being made on the educational system from the perspectives of economic productivity, of democratic citizenship, and of personal fulfillment are convergent" (1996, 10). Convergence is all; contradictions either do not exist or do not matter. Anything that would impose constraints on the power of choice must be either unreal or irrelevant and soon consigned to the past.

Higher education in the United States seems an almost paradigmatic instance of extended choices: choose your type of college or university, choose your school, choose your major, choose your curriculum, choose your classes, and so on. None are inherently right or wrong, as the story goes, but among all the possibilities you will find one exactly right for you. American politics, by contrast, seem a deliberate contraction of choice, imposing a phantom teleology of effects. When choices really matter, when they have immediately visible effects, then multiple possibilities must finally boil down to only two real choices, a good one and a bad one. Small wonder that recent national elections appear to evoke always more intense partisan passions about which is which. Teleology has become one job of an omnivorously two-sided political process, and the effects guaranteed by teleology can be made to seem real only in circumstances of limited choice between the right way and the wrong way.

Neither paradigm of choice can exist by itself, and every institutional formation involves both. Unlimited and proliferating choice in isolation can appear as simply trivializing. If nothing ever happens except more choices, then the results do not matter and competition is just a fraud. Colleges and universities must emphasize the high degree of competitiveness involved with every choice, even in the midst of highlighting the multiple possibilities available. If, however, choice always involves only two options, then freedom seems restricted and competition becomes war. Representations of the border wars between liberal tendencies toward proliferating choices and conservative tendencies toward a two-sided teleology of effects are good illustrations of the political process in the United States, which then predictably occasions more calls for more choices than the extremes of these positions. The intensification of competition around dominant and subordinate class processes depends on constantly intensifying choice both ways: more proliferation, more choices; simultaneously, your choice must come down to this or that.

Thinking about these paradigmatic extremes of choice can help explain a great deal about the affective dynamics of class processes. Hyperindividualism requires very different configurations from what is required for the production of skilled labor. Dominant emotional investments in the agency of "the winner" necessitate a representation of subordinate groups as an undifferentiated mass. In contrast to the elaborate hierarchies characteristic of merit ideologies and the like, hyperindividualist agency appears as agency at all only to the extent it seems a visible origin of an accelerated flow of effects standing out in stark contrast from the undifferentiated, static mass. Any contact across that divide might diminish the isolated visibility of the competitively winning position. Even the noblesse oblige of the winner that appears so often in sports interviews, for example, emphasizes distance, not contact. Winning agency must stand out as if inherent in the winner who is dramatically different from the others, even at the edges, no matter what tiny margin or what contingent circumstances initially separated out the winner. Winning, in other words, requires that every choice be made to seem a fateful, defining event fraught with potential effects. Ultimately, your only real choices are that you can choose to win or you can choose to lose.

The actual production of skilled labor in contrast requires contiguity and continuities. As I argued earlier, waste labor is not a reserve army available in mass for unskilled labor. Waste is the repository of long hours of educational labor *of exactly the same kind as winning agency*, and likewise spread across a considerable spectrum of skills. It must be in order to step into whatever sequence of needs in production. Thus it is not "congealed" labor either, but rather a kind of labor time temporarily depotentiated, as it were, awaiting its hail into production time as required. In contrast to the affective dynamics of hyperindividualism, where winning and losing positions are made to depend on the distance of undifferentiated mass and spotlighted winning agency, in labor terms virtually seamless contact is the key. Waste labor and winner, subordinate class processes and dominant hyperindividualism, must occupy contiguous spaces continuously. In the midst of waste labor, choices are then represented as if endlessly possible, endlessly proliferating. Any corner you turn or any choice you make could suddenly and without warning precipitate you into that other realm of winning agency.

Class processes thus impose a contradictory double burden on postsecondary schools. On one hand, the emotional intensities of hyperindividualism require the elaborate, extended rituals of competition to produce the required affect of distance. As I argue in chapter 5, competition must appear everywhere and be made to seem the natural and normal state of affairs. Whatever minute interval on the occasion separates gold from silver, A from A-, corporate fast track from downsized, and so on, winning position must seem deserved. It must have involved just that little bit extra of competitive fire and innovation—the right choice. On the other hand, waste labor can be mobilized effectively only if produced immediately adjacent to the identifications of winning agency. Competition is everything, but it is also reversible on any given occasion, when waste labor is tapped and "someone" is individuated into agency.

Relative importance and direction, toward foregrounding the affective dynamics of a dominant class hyperindividualism or toward acquiring the skills necessary to a subordinate-class waste labor mass, can vary a great deal from one institution to another, and often from program to program within the same institution. But you will never find an educational institution promising to make every student into a perfectly skilled nonentity within a mass of potential workers, any more than you will find television commercials advertising their product as guaranteeing anonymity and protection from the curse of standing out from the crowd. Conversely, not even the most prestigious universities offer unrestricted money back options if you do not in fact take your degree directly into the position of splendidly isolated winner. Both those contradictory class imperatives, toward distance and toward contiguity, must be continually sustained. Within the terms of class processes educational resolution is impossible. Management thus becomes an ongoing necessity. These conditions imposed on management account for two of the most remarked-on changes in colleges and universities during the 1990s and into the new century: the proliferation of internal assessment procedures, often only vaguely connected to external objectives, and the growth of administration relative to both faculty and students.

It seems a truism to say that research universities have close ties to corporations. In *The Knowledge Factory* (2000), Stanley Aronowitz pushes the point still further to claim an increasing corporatization of university organization, an argument that has been echoed in a number of ways. Yet, as Slaughter and Rhoades point out, the growth in university administration contrasts sharply with typical corporate employment patterns during that same period: "In contrast to the pattern in industry, where the numbers of middle managers have declined, colleges and universities have greatly expanded middle management, whether to supervise commercial endeavor and engagement with various external communities or to support students and information technology." The result is that "institutional expenditures for administration go up, while expenditures for teaching go down" (2004, 332). In an essay entitled "The Associate Vice Provost in the Gray Flannel Suit: Administrative Labor and the Corporate University," Jeffrey Nealon is even more emphatic:

> In the wake of the savage realignment of the 1980s and 1990s, the *last* thing you want to be in today's economy is a middle manager, hopelessly "entrenched" among other levels of stagnated, slow administration—a sitting duck for downsizing. Unless, that is, you work in *university* administration. A recent study shows that between 1975 and 1993 (roughly, the leveraged buyout years), student population increased in American higher education by 28%, "while non-teaching administration increased in personnel by 83 percent" (White and Hauck 2000, 163–164). The NEA offers slightly different numbers for its study of the period 1976–1995, but it offers a similar conclusion. (2007, 95–96)

That NEA study is available online, and, as Nealon adds in a footnote, it also points out that physical plant and clerical hiring have decreased dramatically. Kevin Kniffen's essay "Give Me a $: Moonlighting in the Company Boardroom" (2000) uses a study conducted by Karen Heller and Lily Eng for the *Philadelphia Inquirer* in 1996 that began by noting the startling increase in administrators at the University of Pennsylvania. More than 1,800 of them were added between 1980 and 1996, while the number of students had increased by 29.

The paradox, then, has to do with how academic capitalism seems to link universities more closely than ever to corporate and other external interests, while meanwhile university organizational structure would appear to have changed in almost the opposite direction from corporations, adding rather than eliminating middle management positions. Slaughter and Rhoades attempt to explain the anomaly as involving how university administrators must "supervise commercial endeavor and engagement with various external communities" and "support students and information technology." But dealing with external communities and supporting information technology is hardly unique to university administrators; neither is "commercial endeavor" unheard of in corporations, even if it has increased in universities. Corporate management is not saddled with providing support for students, but then administrators in the university rarely supply much by way of a support structure for students either. That task mostly falls to instructors in the classroom and staff outside it. Multiple layers of administration are daily occupied, however, in the process of overseeing the performances of students, staff, and faculty, assessing the parameters of performance, ensuring at least some exoskeletal structural equity across curricular and degree requirements in different disciplines and programs, regulating the data flow generated by all these processes, and so on.

Even at top-tier research universities where tenured faculty have considerable freedom and autonomy, one need only think, for example, of what is required by the changes in the evaluation of teaching over the last two or three decades. From being almost nonexistent in these research institutions, evaluation has burgeoned to include not only student numbers, but also peer reviews, syllabi and statements about courses, portfolios from sample students, and so on. Administrators must oversee how each step is designed, monitored, and assessed as successful or not, and then the accumulated data must be interpreted longitudinally as well as on the occasion of each class taught by each faculty member in the process of merit review. Overseeing part-time and temporary faculty has always been assumed to require considerable assessment time, and the growing numbers in these categories together with the dramatic increase in assessment has pushed the amount exponentially. Writing instructors are a large segment of part-time and temporary faculty, with the result, as Donna Strickland points out in "The Managerial Unconscious of Composition Studies," that anyone hired into a tenure-track rhetoric or composition position can expect to walk straight into administrative work: "While junior faculty in literature are hired primarily to teach and—depending on the institution—to conduct research, composition specialists are hired to do these things *and* to direct and develop programs, either immediately or in the near future" (2003, 46; Strickland's emphasis).

It is true that any corporate management must be involved in assessment, and very often results are kept strictly in-house. Nevertheless, assessment in most corporations is ultimately directed at outcomes external to the corporation. That is, the effects of assessment procedures are assumed to occur elsewhere, and to circuit back into the corporate structure by way of a range of other sites affected in various ways. While this happens also with the results of college and university assessments, from student grades going elsewhere to data for legislative budget committees, an astonishing amount remains a matter primarily of internal processes connected in only the most tangential way with outcomes that might register externally. The most crucial effects are internal and ship outside only as part of a more or less already completely managed package.

Rather than direct outcomes, the elaborate machinery of multiple assessment practices produces the necessarily double yield required of management by class processes. Assessment attempts to legitimize competitive distance for the winners in whatever evaluative grids *and* simultaneously to ensure the equally complex skills necessary across the board to produce as large as possible a labor resource. In short, it falls primarily to the range of university middle management and its assessment imperatives to provide the middle ground that both manages and sustains the contradictory imperatives imposed by class processes. Waste labor conditions for exploitation must be produced, while at the same time the upper reaches of university education can be persistently symbolized as the producer of highly successfully competitive individuals, distinguished from others at this peak of success.

Management functions intensify the lower down the scale of faculty prestige and the more involvement with undergraduate teaching. As I argue in chapter 5, control of labor is exercised primarily by the power to hire and fire rather than by some scientific management–like total reorganization and regimentation of daily work practices. Postdoctoral students assigned to teaching and part-time and temporary faculty are most vulnerable to firing, but they must also be skilled and available to be hired on short notice when it seems necessary or possible. Firing can be justified on budget grounds, which may require some considerable administrative finesse, but also on performance grounds that will certainly require elaborate performance records to justify. Rehiring personnel will likely require equal justification of reasons to expect upgraded performance. Lower-level instructors are typically assigned to teach lower-level students, who in turn require considerably more supervision and stricter assessment parameters, just as lower-level faculty members require more assessment from lower-level managers. Almost inevitably the greatest points of tension occur at intersections across different levels, for example, when students transfer into research universities having satisfied a writing requirement in a basic writing course outsourced to a nearby community college, or when instructors have at best only rudimentary ESL experience and still must deal with large numbers of nonnative speakers of English in their classes.

Nealon satirizes the idea that "administration-think" will guarantee the future health of universities: "The line of thinking seems to go something like this: in responding to the challenges of the twenty-first century, universities finally require more management—part-time instructors ruthlessly overseen, post-tenure review for full-time faculty, and more intensive testing for students. Intensified administration, in short, seems to be the prescription for the future health of higher education" (2007, 103). Aronowitz goes even further, arguing that a separate class of administrators have subverted the basic learning processes of the university: "The learning enterprise has become subject to the growing power of administration, which more and more responds not to faculty and students, except at the margins, but to political and corporate forces that claim sovereignty over higher education" (2000, 164). When administrators look outward to "political and corporate forces," however, it is usually at the request of faculty, as Slaughter and Rhoades argue persuasively. Administration proliferates, and administrative functions performed by faculty and staff proliferate, in relation to the contradictory imperatives imposed by class processes requiring a continual intensification of administration. Whatever administrative management is supplied never seems quite enough. In the circumstances I have been describing, more management of some form or another will always appear as if a necessity.

Rather than be entirely turned over to a separate class of administrators, as Aronowitz sometimes implies, much of the lower-level daily work of management is actually performed by faculty, often as a partial course release from extremely heavy teaching loads for lecturers and other non-tenured faculty. Fewer faculty in the classroom means more part-time and temporary hires to replace them. Students meanwhile must pay for more and more of their college education even as it gets more expensive. Still, most students have high expectations for getting a degree and for the rewards it is supposed to bring, even though, as James Rosenbaum's data suggest in *Beyond College for All*, most have little real knowledge at all of what exactly they will be required to do in college or what will likely happen to them. Generalizing from the results of surveys and interviews, Rosenbaum reports that while still in high school "students can see the college enrollment of last year's seniors more easily than the college completion of much older students, and they can more easily identify with the students a year older than themselves who enter college than with the twenty-eight-year-olds who never finished the degree. As a result, their perceptions are likely to be distorted" (2001, 81). High-school performance can seem basically irrelevant to admission success, and the idea of having to build on knowledge and work habits acquired in high school never quite takes hold.

It is often the case that high-school teachers and counselors encourage the perception of having to work hard in intensely competitive circumstances in college. After all, the against-all-odds emotional dynamics of class processes requires a way to "choose success" as if a visible and isolated apex, something available only to those rare few (with whom everyone identifies) willing to make the sacrifices and do the extra work. Shorn of this mysticism of heroic effort, however, the actual work that fills up daily labor time is rarely anticipated or explained. Composition instructors, for example, know how reluctant students are about doing revisions that obviously extend the time involved. Likewise, the complex relations between that daily labor of whatever sort and the various evaluative grids in which it is inserted are often unclear to students, even in circumstances where "grading standards" for a specific test or paper in a specific class are spelled out. For that grade is only a very small part of the process of expanded grading I describe in chapter 5. It simply notches into the complicated assessment procedures involved in the managerial balancing act required by class processes.

Nealon agrees with Slaughter and Rhoades that the humanities lose out under the academic capitalism of the entrepreneurial university. As he memorably puts it, "While some of the hard sciences got the goldmine as a consequence of university corporatization since the 1980s, most of the humanities got the shaft" (94). In one sense this is nothing new; the humanities are never funded on the same scale as the sciences or the professional schools. As even the sciences are scaled out by relative proximity to immediate markets for research, however, it is not impossible to imagine things getting much worse for the humanities. Demand from external constituencies and from other disciplines in the university seems highest for writing, basic language instruction, and communication skills generally—the most immediately visible aspects of literacy training. But within the humanities these areas have traditionally been viewed as "service" or "vocational" oriented, and the training of undergraduates has been assigned to the lowest level of instructors, usually graduate assistants or temporary appointments. Thus the unhappy alternatives are likely to appear as either succumbing completely to this perceived vocationalizing of undergraduate education or attempting somehow the difficulties of the academic capitalism of upper-level research with the necessity it imposes to find some entrance into an off-campus market for more privileged elements of the humanities. No wonder aging donors who fondly remember their undergraduate Shakespeare course are relentlessly canvassed for bequests, named chairs and the like.

These contradictory imperatives of management do not really constitute a "crisis." Unless and until class processes change dramatically in relation to educational functions, postsecondary student training will involve large-scale academic management largely located with disciplines and institutions identified as "teaching." As literacy practices associated with the cultural capital of literature and textual studies are gradually being replaced by the different sets of literacy practices involved in management imperatives, however, attempts to challenge and to build alternatives to dominant structures must be imagined in different ways. In retrospect, it seems easy enough to be dismissive about the theory-driven claims for "ideological critique" that began appearing frequently, in a number of different forms, during the 1980s. Nevertheless, because unavoidably articulated and practiced in relation to dominant literacies and their cultural capital, those critiques did help to open and to reshape educational pathways for a great many students. That will not continue to be the case given the dominance of management imperatives, however, making it all the more important to understand what has changed in order to point alternative directions in these new circumstances as well.

From Roger Kimball through David Horowitz, conservative attacks on academia typically targeted "tenured radicals" in both the humanities and the social sciences for promoting theories that undermine "basic" assumptions. Doubtless such attacks will continue, but in contrast to the Kimball/Horowitz line, David Brooks argues in his recent *On Paradise Drive* that both today's students and today's capitalism find the radicals who exercised conservatives in the 1980s as now just a kind of common sense: "These notions may have been promulgated by people who thought of themselves as radicals. . . . But they are perfectly suited to the ethos of the achievement oriented capitalist. . . . The world of floating signifiers and upended cultural hierarchies . . . is a world of maximum fluidity and flexibility: just the sort of world the opportunity-seeking meritocrat wants to live in" (2004, 161). What worries Brooks about university education is not tenured radicals, but the absence of a much older educational imperative to build character: "Although today's colleges impose all sorts of rules to reduce safety risks and encourage achievement, they see passing along knowledge, not building character, as their primary task. If you ask professors whether they seek to instill character, they often look at you blankly. They are on campus to instill calculus, or nineteenth-century history, or whatever their academic specialty happens to be" (2004, 175). In sum, Brooks argues that rather than waste time attacking tenured radicals, conservatives should put their energy into a management process that goes well beyond the mere transmission of knowledge toward the end of building character.

Brooks has no interest in trying systematically to link the "achievement oriented capitalist" and the "opportunity-seeking meritocrat" he criticizes to the competitive intensities of neoliberalism, let alone anything like the larger processes of class formation. Yet unlike a number of other conservatives who follow a more economistic neoliberalism emphasizing rational choice and direction, he recognizes with the vocational education reformers discussed in chapter 2 that building character should be integrated with imaginative development and skill training. Like them, he frequently invokes much earlier educational traditions. Whereas vocational-education reformers such as Resnick and Wirt point to Horace Mann or John Dewey, Brooks has rather different ideas in mind, and decidedly different figures from the past: "It is interesting, by way of comparison, to go back a century or so ago, before the code of the meritocrat had fully established its hegemony over education and life. The most striking contrast between the college atmosphere of those days and these is that collegians then were relatively unconcerned with grades and academic achievements, but they lived in a web of moral instruction" (2004, 176). John Hibben, Princeton president in the first two decades of the twentieth century, appears a particular favorite because of his devotion to character building and morality, and his significant attention to the devil in his addresses to Princeton students. "Today the blue bloods are gone," Brooks admits, "and nobody wants them to return. We live in a much fairer society—one in which education is spread more broadly, so that the numbers of students at Ohio State and the University of Texas dwarf the numbers in the Ivy League schools. Still the Hibbenses of the old aristocracy did take the system they were born into and articulate a public moral language, the language of chivalry and noblesse oblige. They did create activities and institutions designed to instill character" (2004, 178–179).

There may be something terrifying for a conservative imaginary in contemplating the possibility of radicals haranguing packed lecture halls of students required to listen. Thinking like Brooks, however, could well introduce another location into a conservative agenda, with more positive possibilities for conservatives (and frightening possibilities for the rest of us) than endless attacks on campus radicals. With their small classrooms that feature daily personal interactions, writing-program composition courses can easily be identified as the ideal alternative to suit Brooks's purposes of character building. Brooks suggests that tenured faculty will not want to bother, but composition instruction is carried out by a vast teaching workforce often holding at best very precarious positions, already directly subject to an immense variety of management imperatives, and usually in no circumstances to present a powerfully effective counter. In addition, what Richard Miller refers to as composition's self-understanding can be recognized as quite close to the classroom environment Brooks would wish for as an experiment in building character, if not necessarily to his politics by any means: "Indeed, it is safe to say that Composition understands itself to be and would like to be understood by others as *the* institutional preserve of sound pedagogical practice. We are the ones who are interested in process, not product. We are the ones who have student-centered rather than content-driven courses. And we are the ones committed to thinking and learning, equal access, group work, collaboration, and all the other pillars that support the democratic ideal" (2001, 25). With the emphasis on student-centered pedagogy rather than on transmitting knowledge, composition classrooms could well be imagined as places to build character in Brooks's quite different understanding of what that involves.

In addition to the potential of class size and course content that could be made to function toward the ideological mobilization Brooks imagine, composition courses already feature importantly in what might be understood as a kind of structural management of student movement through educational institutions. Unlike the clearly demarcated dual tracks typical in secondary schools in the past, undergraduate education at almost any given institution might operate simultaneously as a fast track to graduate and professional schools, vocational training, and part of a mazy network of postsecondary programs in multiple locations. Among other things, however, this means that within that mix, as it varies from one institution to another, various sectors supply a kind of de facto tracking. Rather than elaborate hierarchies or designated "flunk out" courses as in the past, the tracking is now often done by means of accelerating or slowing student flow toward a degree, where writing instruction plays a central role. Individual students perceived as in need of more writing instruction than their peers are often targeted toward lower-level vocational preparation rather than graduate degrees or professional school. As a result of being held for more requirements, passage to degree becomes slower, and often students drop out. The more writing instruction you need to write proficiently, the more directly oriented toward lower-level vocations your undergraduate education will likely become, and the more likely it is that you end up at community colleges or in certificate programs as a final level of education.

At very top-tier research schools, the fast track tends to be the most visible part of undergraduate education, but Slaughter and Rhoades argue that "the majority of four-year colleges and universities as well as community colleges interact with the new economy in a more mundane fashion. Corporations in the new economy require well-educated workers in business-related areas—science, engineering, medicine, law—to create and protect knowledge-based products, processes and services. Corporations also need employees able to deal with the high-technology products and services characteristic of the new economy. At the undergraduate level, business has become the core curricula. The majority of all courses taken in four-year schools are in business fields" (303). Business fields thus become the largest in-house client in need of writing instruction for their students, and they tend to dominate one side of the complicated boundary zone between the humanities and other disciplines. Because of the labor organization of the humanities, however, extensive daily interaction in that boundary zone is rarely shaped from the other side by tenured faculty in disciplines such as English, except for those who specialize in composition. Aside from composition specialists aware of a great deal of research in fields such as Writing Across the Curriculum, most tenured faculty have little knowledge of what other disciplines expect from writing instruction.

Yet university management logic works on the premise that the more teaching-intensive the area, the more administrative management is required, particularly when, as in writing instruction, the workforce is largely made up of graduate teaching assistants, postdoctoral students, and instructors on temporary appointments of one kind or another. Many critics have noted the recent proliferation of jobs available to those with advanced degrees in some area of composition theory or rhetoric, unlike what is available for most fields in English or generally in the humanities. While the jobs now seem plentiful and research possibilities more available, one of the key points made by Marc Bousquet "is that persons holding the rhet-comp Ph.D. will frequently expect to serve the managed university *as management*" (2003, 3). In contrast, the instructors "whose labor is overseen by the holder of the rhet-comp Ph.D. are commonly persons who have experience of graduate study in other fields of English—current or former graduate students working as flexible labor, rather than as colleagues" (ibid.). As textual scholarship in disciplines such as English retreats farther and farther from any kind of reading instruction that might work in tandem with the actual conditions of writing instruction, these disciplines continue to ensure an oversupply of "disposable teachers," while "rhet-comp" doctoral programs supply the management.

Bousquet challenges the contention of James Porter and Patricia Sullivan that writing-program administrators have functioned effectively to improve teaching conditions and expand the job market for PhDs in composition: "The discipline's enormous usefulness to academic capitalism—in delivering cheap teaching, training a supervisory stratum, and producing a group of intellectuals theorizing and legitimizing this scene of managed labor—has to be given at least as much credit in this expansion as the heroic efforts that Porter and Sullivan call the WPA's 'strong track record for enacting change'" (2000, 17). Bousquet argues that tenured and tenure-track rhetoric-composition faculty have instead directly or indirectly cooperated with management imperatives under the sign of a necessary "pragmatism:" "Representing corporate dominance as a fact of life, this brand of pragmatism ultimately conceals a historically specific ideological orientation (neoliberalism) behind an aggressive (re)description of reality, in which left-wing bogeymen are sometimes raised as the threats to human agency" (2003, 26).

Predictably enough, when Bousquet's argument was first circulated it attracted considerable controversy on the WPA listserv and elsewhere. Many felt so-called pragmatic accommodation well worth it after years in which those in the field had been uniformly treated as second-class citizens at best. These conceptions of pragmatism, however, can slip very easily into a neoliberal fantasy of choice, as if one is empowered from the beginning to stand outside and make decisions about where and when to join up. Nevertheless, as the critique of composition's "management" positioning in university organization and the continual referencing of job-market possibilities become something of an internal industry within rhetoric and composition, these arguments risk becoming the very kind of neoliberal ethical contest that Bousquet fears: on one side pragmatic accommodation, and on the other heroic resistance.

The issue is important because in many educational institutions writing instruction occupies the transition zones of a complex ensemble of intersecting class processes. If at the most visible ideological extreme there is a real potential for being forced into the role of character police for conservative politics, writing instruction has already become a primary agent for the acceleration or deceleration of students into the workforce. Positionally, as a part of vocational training, writing classrooms in a great many different institutional forms also have connections into the immense group of dropout students and unemployed adults. Finally, an increasingly larger group of more or less permanent faculty specializing in some area of rhetoric and composition are put in the position of carrying out many of the everyday details of managerial administrative required of higher educational institutions by the double operations of class processes I described earlier. Meanwhile, the teaching of writing largely falls to the disposable teachers produced by PhD programs in English and other disciplines of the humanities.

My examples of management and management issues point toward future directions that seem to me imperative to consider now. Most immediately, in the corporate university driven by the kind of academic capitalism that Slaughter and Rhoades describe, it is necessary to understand much more than most of us do about other disciplinary practices. I do not mean the usual litanies about "interdisciplinary" knowledge, or even the disciplines that usually appear under that umbrella in the humanities. If, as Slaughter and Rhoades point out, business programs of one kind or another occupy huge numbers of students and credits, then the many forms of business literacy should become primary subject matter. I argued earlier that "literacy" could not really become an area of study in the same way as eighteenth-century English literature or even textual studies generally. Specific *literacies*, however, require research and careful understanding. That knowledge is a necessary part of understanding where our students are going when they leave our classes, what they are doing there and why, what organizes their labor, and what pressures can be exerted on those conditions from outside. In turn, it is part of how we can educate students, for example, by teaching counter economic literacies to a dominant neoliberal model, as I argue in my article "Just Choose: Derivative Education as Economic Literacy" (2006).

My image of David Brooks in the composition classroom offers a different kind of example, although here as well ongoing literacy research can prove useful, particularly research in multimodal literacy as linked with the study of specific technologies. "The Decline of the Book" is a well-worn lament of textual scholars in humanities disciplines, but new technologies have made books obsolete about as much as computers made offices paperless. It is not necessarily that "the book" is in danger of disappearing, but rather that a range of academic interpretive practices in the humanities, still involving relatively very select groups of texts, seems increasingly disconnected from anything resembling the everyday practices of most students most of the time. And contrary to much "crisis" discussion along the lines of David Laurence's address that I quoted earlier, you cannot get people to "realize the value" of interpreting texts simply by making them do it over and over again. In contrast, one of the most frequent themes of literacy research as well as a great deal of composition theory involves the recognition of student-centered *production* as a key feature of both student relations to technology and the classrooms that occupy their educational time.

There is nothing inherently transformative about such a shift from interpretation to production, or, as the familiar composition mantra has it, putting students rather than texts at the center of the classroom. "Production" in this or any other context involves labor, and no one can convert classrooms into "a good thing" à la Martha Stewart just by invoking student production. As labor, there is every reason to understand as much as possible about what goes on under the names of both "production" and "interpretation." Nevertheless, besides its familiar coordinates to most students, there seems to me a kind of strategic use in thinking first toward the idea of student production in the classroom. The Brooks example suggests among other things that the labor at issue will likely involve the labor on the self, for his purposes the process of "building character," and it is initially easier to see what that involves by thinking first in terms of what exactly this production process is all about. In a larger context, I argue in chapter 2 that new selves became a crucially central topic in conceptions of vocational education reform, and indeed the idea of producing working selves had been important throughout the history of vocational education.

Finally, it seems to me especially important to rethink for educational and political ends the whole complex of issues around the growth of educational administration. Despite the critique of administration by Aronowitz (and nearly everyone else in the humanities, it would seem) and the critiques of management such as Nealon's and my own, and Bousquet's and a number of others in composition, all this will not go away as a result. I do not mean to sound like Bousquet's would-be pragmatist, who argues that the process of managing academic labor is a "fact of life" to which we must accommodate ourselves. I mean something more on the order of Harkin's response to Laurence that I quoted earlier in this chapter, if on a rather lower frequency. Management imperatives are driven by class processes, and they will not disappear from educational institutions even if everybody in the humanities repeated over and over every day that management is really, really bad shit. That may be a consensus indeed, but it is the kind of consensus Laurence fantasizes rather than the development of collective direction.

Class processes may impose the impossible burdens of managing the formation of labor forces, but in so doing they also introduce into the humanities the potential for collective organization in a way that has not existed on such a scale before. Because it was tied to the institutional growth of humanities disciplines such as English during the twentieth century, textual studies as a dominant model of research and teaching was always positioned as a privatizing practice. It was at once dependent on and expected to augment the reserves of cultural capital feeding growth, while at the same time hiding the necessary exploitation of lower-level workers assigned to "service" courses yielding huge numbers of student credit hours. Thus, over the last few decades, anyone intent on challenging dominant norms of textual study has had first to face in one way or another the immense work of deprivatizing interpretive practices just in order to begin opening up other and more public social spaces of inquiry. Even more significantly, those in writing programs, for example, designated by dominant models of textual studies as merely service providers, could realize possibilities of collectivity only in relatively isolated pockets. Management can surely be privatizing, as Aronowitz's critique of the development of a separate class of administrators shows quite clearly. At some level, however, the process of institutionally managing academic labor requires a kind of collectivity. After all, the existence of that separate class Aronowitz critiques depends completely on the immense and complex layering networks of lower-level managers.

Management in any case can be realized in a number of different forms. To take the obvious large example, labor unions as they developed through the first half of the twentieth century were actively engaged in managing labor and the formation of labor forces in a great many different ways. Historically, all kinds of worker groups and worker councils have existed to manage labor in collective terms, sometimes in ways that benefited all the workers and sometimes not. Trying directly to import any specific organization from the past is unlikely to work well in current conditions, but it is always worth the reminder that existing ways of doing things are neither timeless nor "for the best." In thinking about possible collective directions, I very much like Bousquet's response to my argument in "Managing Comp" about constructing political alliances in the circumstances of academic work: "My problem here [with Watkins's argument] is that the 'groups' of composition management and labor are not just 'differently' positioned, but instead *specifically* positioned in a definable and traceable relation of exploitation" (2002, 921). His critique of my "differently" seems to me entirely justified. My qualification, however, is that it is a mistake to imagine the positioning he describes as a matter of "management" on one side and "labor" on the other. Not because some composition managers may be pretty good guys after all, but because the division reproduces an already very familiar model in composition studies that Peggy O'Neill in fact turned against Bousquet himself.

In "Unpacking Assumptions, Providing Context: A Response to Marc Bousquet," O'Neill argues that Bousquet "neglects to mention the well-documented contentious relationship between composition and literary studies. . . . Failure to acknowledge the deep and divisive relationship between these two areas demonstrates a failure to understand the work of

WPAs, writing instructors, and composition scholars as well as the scholarship and professional realities of the field" (2002, 910). I seriously doubt that Bousquet would deny the effects on composition of the dominance of literary studies, especially the forms of exploitation I suggested earlier. But understanding that exploitation is not quite the same as O'Neill's image of a "contentious relationship" between the "good labor" of comp instructors just interested in "quality work" (2002, 912) on one side and their managers in literary study on the other. Assuming some absolute divide between labor/management in the circumstances of academic work—whether in O'Neill's version or in Bousquet's own—seems to me a dead end, especially now. One of the general lessons I would draw from focusing on vocational education reform as I have is that if you are teaching in a postsecondary institution in the United States, you are also engaged in vocational training. And if you are engaged in the work of vocational training, you are also engaged in the managing of labor. I intend the emphasis to reinforce Bousquet's point about the specifics of positioning and the relations of exploitation, by extending it to the recognition that you cannot cut cleanly through all that as if it were simply a labor/management division.

As Nealon points out, tenured faculty in research institutions are likely nevertheless to try, if from a very different perspective from Bousquet's: "In my experience, most tenure-track faculty members want absolutely nothing to do with the administrative functions of the university, and many restrict their involvement with those functions to complaining bitterly about work they've left others to perform: 'Why are my classes so overfull? Who admitted these unprepared students? Where's my new computer, my raise, or my travel funding?'" (2007, 98). Unlike Nealon, I might not characterize the reason behind all this as a matter of faculty "responsibility for the abrogation of their sovereignty" as corporate administration grew. That kind of "sovereignty" seems to me rather more likely to have been a part of a Bill Readings–inspired university-somewhere-in-a-past-that-never-existed and hence not really available to shirk. The more crucial point, however, is that complaints such as those that Nealon criticizes are often driven by the much larger assumption (in both left and right political versions) that humanities disciplines could function as direct alternatives to the service pragmatism of writing instruction or even as pockets of alternative education within increasingly corporatized and vocational-oriented colleges and universities driven by market forces. Somehow, just by doing what we do and being what we are as disciplines, we offer alternatives. Yet, no matter what we imagine on the inside, in circumstances of a burgeoning academic capitalism, that imaginary of would-be alternatives points to something more accurately described as user-friendly niche markets.

In limited terms, such markets might make up for the loss of cultural capital reserves by being custom-programmed in a way that would make them attractive to university administrations. Even large departments such as English could become much smaller, in order to offer an upmarket luxury good. For those students who can afford college, who have the credentials, and who are relatively well placed in terms of moving through a job-training curriculum, literary study in English could provide a more rounded claim for possessing communication skills while also allowing the pleasures of developing interests in a wide range of literature. For colleges and universities in an intensely competitive environment, eager to create a unique brand name and to craft each entering class in its image, literary study might well become a crucial factor in the total package. As a welcome addition to all those promotional posters Ernest Boyer noticed that feature endlessly sunny campuses with students in class under the spreading trees by the water, you could zoom the texts of Milton and Morrison right alongside the iPods and laptops. Not a happy vision, I would hope, but that is what happens to alternatives imagined as if a separate existence. They become basic food for dominant class processes.

I do not find the vision of being positioned instead as a part of postsecondary vocational training intrinsically horrific at all. As I suggested earlier, understanding the immense complexity of contemporary literacies and their historical sources seems to me a significantly important future direction in part because they are closely linked to the skills embedded in that vocational training. Literacy research in this sense connects directly to classroom practices in ways that affect huge numbers of students. Attempts at transforming class-imposed imperatives into new forms of collective management and new worker coalitions are already an ongoing reality, and one that can be pursued much further. I have argued throughout this book that the fantasy of vocational-education reformers in the 1980s and 1990s that a new economy would somehow create model egalitarian workplaces was actually realized instead in the emergence of new processes of class formation that extended relations of exploitation. Once you lose the reformers' assumptions about the magic of the economy, however, an idea of egalitarian workplaces seems to me a fantasy worth working for in current conditions of postsecondary institutions. Vocational-education reformers did a great deal to unlock the systems of Prosserized efficiency running vocational training. They may have fantasized a lot about the "new" economy, but they also attempted to introduce into what had been closed curricula ways of thinking critically about citizenship, about politics, and about cultural production in relation to economic issues. Most important, they understood the introduction of those directions of study as connected to rather than somehow an alternative to or opposed to vocational training.

It is true enough that class processes have always been at home in vocational education. For those of us teaching in colleges and universities, that home is no longer—if it ever really was—somewhere else. Rather than lament some imaginary of better days, it is worth trying to expand what vocational reformers initiated by working to rethink labor and all its complex of associated social networks. Being positioned within class division and exploitation does not signal the impossibility of imagining a social world beyond that. It does mean that we can and must find ways to use where we are for bringing it into being.

REFERENCES

Aronowitz, Stanley. *The Knowledge Factory: Dismantling the Corporate University and Creating True Higher Learning.* Boston, 2000.
Augustine, Curt. Letter to the editor. *Sacramento Bee*, May 16, 2002.
Barone, Michael. *Hard America, Soft America: Competition vs. Coddling and the Battle for the Nation's Future.* New York, 2004.
Blank, William. "Future Perspectives in Vocational Education." In Pautler, *Workforce Education*, 281–289.
Bourdieu, Pierre. *Distinction: A Social Critique of the Judgment of Taste.* Trans. Richard Nice. Cambridge, Mass., 1984.
Bousquet, Marc. "Composition as Management Science." In Bousquet, Scott, and Parascondola, *Tenured Bosses and Disposable Teachers*, 11–35.
———. "A Discipline Where Only Management Gets Tenure?" *JAC* 22, no. 4 (2002): 917–925.
Bousquet, Marc, Tony Scott, and Leo Parascondola, eds. *Tenured Bosses and Disposable Teachers: Writing Instruction in the Managed University.* Carbondale, Ill., 2003.
Boyer, Ernest. *College: The Undergraduate Experience in America.* New York, 1987.
Braverman, Harry. *Labor and Monopoly Capital: The Degradation of Work in the Twentieth Century.* New York, 1974.
Bridges, William. "The End of the Job: Seven Rules to Break in a De-Jobbed World." *Fortune* 130 (September 19, 1994).
Brooks, David. *On Paradise Drive: How We Live Now (and Always Have) in the Future Tense.* New York, 2004.
Clark, Burton. *The Open-Door College: A Case Study.* New York, 1960.
———. "The Cooling-Out Function Revisited." *New Directions for Community Colleges* 8 (1980): 15–31.
Craig, John. "The Tech Prep Associate Degree Program." In Pautler, *Workforce Education*, 129–143.
Cubberley, Ellwood. *Changing Conceptions of Education.* Boston, 1909.
Deleuze, Gilles. "Postscript on Control Societies." In *Negotiations*, trans. Martin Joughin, 177–182. New York, 1995.
Deleuze, Gilles, and Felix Guattari. *A Thousand Plateaus: Capitalism and Schizophrenia.* Trans. Brian Massumi. Minneapolis, 1987.

Dewey, John. *Democracy and Education.* New York, 1916.
Duffy, Elizabeth. *Crafting a Class: College Admissions and Financial Aid, 1955–1994.* Princeton, 1998.
Ehrenreich, Barbara. *Fear of Falling: The Inner Life of the Middle Class.* New York, 1989.
Glassman, Ronald. *The New Middle Class and Democracy in a Global Perspective.* New York, 1997.
Gordon, Howard. *The History and Growth of Vocational Education in America.* 2nd ed. Prospect Heights, Ill., 2003.
Gray, Kenneth, and Edwin Herr. *Other Ways to Win: Creating Alternatives for High School Graduates.* Thousand Oaks, Calif., 1995; 2nd ed., 2000.
———. *Workforce Education: The Basics.* Boston, 1998.
Grubb, W. Norton. *Working in the Middle: Strengthening Education and Training for the Mid-Skilled Labor Force.* San Francisco, 1996.
Guillory, John. *Cultural Capital: The Problem of Literary Canon Formation.* Chicago, 1993.
Hardt, Michael, and Antonio Negri. *Empire.* Cambridge, Mass., 2000.
———. *Multitude: War and Democracy in the Age of Empire.* New York, 2004.
Harkin, Patricia. "Response to David Laurence's 'Latest Forecast.'" *CEA Online Forum*, Winter 2003, www.as.ysu.edu/cea.
Hogg, Cheryl. "Vocational Education: Past, Present, and Future." In Pautler, *Workforce Education*, 3–20.
Hull, Dan. *Getting Started in Tech Prep.* Austin, Tex., 1992.
Kitson, Harry. "Trends in Vocational Guidance." In Lee, *Objectives and Problems of Vocational Education*, 257–280.
Kniffin, Kevin. "Give Me a $: Moonlighting in the Corporate Boardroom." In White and Hauck, *Campus, Inc.*, 157–170.
Kumar, Amitava, ed. *Class Issues: Pedagogy, Cultural Studies and the Public Sphere.* New York, 1997.
Laclau, Ernesto, and Chantal Mouffe. *Hegemony and Socialist Strategy.* London, 1985.
Laurence, David. "The Latest Forecast: The Future of the English Profession." *CEA Online Forum*, Winter 2003, www.as.ysu.edu/cea.
Lee, Edwin, ed. *Objectives and Problems of Vocational Education.* 2nd ed. New York, 1938.
Liebow, Elliot. "No Man Can Live with the Terrible Knowledge That He Is Not Needed." *New York Times Magazine*, April 5, 1970.
Lipsitz, George. "Class and Consciousness: Teaching About Social Class in Public Universities." In Kumar, *Class Issues*, 9–21.
Lopez, Kathryn Jean. "If Tinseltown Heads Right." *Sacramento Bee*, July 27, 2007.
Marx, Karl. *Capital: A Critique of Political Economy.* Trans. Ben Fowkes and David Fernbach. New York, 1981.

Miller, Richard. "From Intellectual Wasteland to Resource-Rich Colony: Capitalizing on the Role of Writing Instruction in Higher Education." *Writing Program Administration* 24, no. 3 (2001): 25–40.
National Alliance of Business. *Shaping Tomorrow's Workforce*. Washington, D.C., 1988.
National Center on Education and the Economy. *America's Choice: High Skills or Low Wages!* Washington, D.C., 1990.
Nealon, Jeffrey. "The Associate Vice Provost in the Gray Flannel Suit: Administrative Labor and the Corporate University." *Rethinking Marxism* 19, no. 1 (January 2007): 92–109.
Occupational Outlook Handbook. 1998–99 edition. Indianapolis, 1998.
Occupational Outlook Handbook. 2004–2005 edition. Indianapolis, 2004.
Olson, Lynn. *The School-to-Work Revolution: How Employers and Educators Are Joining Forces to Prepare Tomorrow's Skilled Workforce*. Reading, Mass., 1997.
O'Neill, Peggy. "Unpacking Assumptions, Providing Context: A Response to Marc Bousquet." *JAC* 22, no. 4 (2002): 906–917.
Parnell, Dale. *The Neglected Majority*. Washington, D.C., 1985.
Pautler, Albert, ed. *Workforce Education: Issues for the New Century*. Ann Arbor, Mich., 1999.
Phillips, Kevin. *Arrogant Capital: Washington, Wall Street, and the Frustration of American Politics*. Boston, 1994.
Porter, James, Patricia Sullivan, et al. "Institutional Critique: A Rhetorical Methodology for Change." *CCC* 51 (2000): 610–641.
Prosser, Charles. "A Forecast and a Prophecy." In Lee, *Objectives and Problems of Vocational Education*, 389–415.
Prosser, Charles, and C. R. Allen. *Vocational Education in a Democracy*. New York, 1925.
Reich, Robert. *The Work of Nations: Preparing Ourselves for 21st Century Capitalism*. New York, 1991.
Resnick, Lauren, and John Wirt, eds. *Linking School and Work: Roles for Standards and Assessment*. San Francisco, 1996.
Rifkin, Jeremy. *The End of Work: The Decline of the Global Labor Force and the Dawn of the Post-Market Era*. New York, 1995.
Robbins, Bruce. *Upward Mobility and the Common Good: Toward a Literary History of the Welfare State*. Princeton, 2007.
Rosenbaum, James. *Beyond College for All: Career Paths for the Forgotten Half*. New York, 2001.
Secretary's Commission on Achieving Necessary Skills. *What Work Requires of Schools: A SCANS Report for America 2000*. Washington, D.C., 1991.
———. *Learning a Living: A Blueprint for High Performance: A SCANS Report for America 2000*. Washington, D.C., 1992.
———. *Skills and Tasks for Jobs: A SCANS Report for America 2000*. Washington, D.C., 1992.

Slaughter, Sheila, and Larry Leslie. *Academic Capitalism: Politics, Policies and the Entrepreneurial University*. Baltimore, 1997.

Slaughter, Sheila, and Gary Rhoades. *Academic Capitalism and the New Economy: Markets, State, and Higher Education*. Baltimore, 2004.

Strange, Susan. *Casino Capitalism*. New York, 1986.

Strickland, Donna. "The Managerial Unconscious of Composition Studies." In Bousquet, Scott, and Parascondola, *Tenured Bosses and Disposable Teachers*, 46–56.

Strobel, Frederick, and Wallace Peterson. *The Coming Class War and How to Avoid It: Rebuilding the American Middle Class*. Armonk, N.Y., 1999.

Super, Donald. *Career Education and the Meaning of Work*. Washington, D.C., 1976.

Taylor, Frederick. *Scientific Management*. New York, 1947.

Tucker, Marc. "Skills Standards, Qualifications Systems, and the American Workforce." In Resnick and Wirt, *Linking School and Work: Roles for Standards and Assessment*, 23–51.

Violas, Paul. *The Training of the Urban Working Class*. Chicago, 1978.

Watkins, Evan. *Everyday Exchanges: Marketwork and Capitalist Common Sense*. Stanford, Calif., 1998.

———. "Managing Comp." *JAC* 22, no. 4 (2002): 899–906.

———. "Just Choose: Derivative Literacy as Economic Education." *JAC* 26, nos. 3–4 (2006): 585–600.

Weir, Margaret, ed. *The Social Divide: Political Parties and the Future of Activist Government*. Washington, D.C., 1998.

White, Geoffrey, and Flannery Hauck, eds. *Campus, Inc.: Corporate Power in the Ivory Tower*. Amherst, N.Y., 2000.

Wolfe, Alan. *One Nation After All: What Middle-Class Americans Really Think About God, Country, Family, Racism, Welfare, Immigration, Homosexuality, Work, the Right, the Left, and Each Other*. New York, 1998.

Wolff, Richard, and Stephen Resnick. *Knowledge and Class: A Marxian Critique of Political Economy*. Chicago, 1987.

INDEX

Academic, separation from vocational track, 2–4, 13–14, 44–45, 50, 57
Academic capitalism, 15–16, 75, 80, 92–94, 96, 103, 107, 111–12, 117
Administration, university, 102–3, 105, 114, 116–17
Against-all-odds plots, 2–8, 10, 12, 14, 44, 60, 70, 84, 91, 106
Alger, Horatio, 2, 5
Allen, C. R., 18, 47
American Association of Junior and Community Colleges, 48
American Vocational Association, 4, 37
America's Choice: High Skills or Low Wages!, 7, 26, 50
Aronowitz, Stanley, 102, 105–6, 114–15
Assessment practices, 27, 69, 89, 102, 104–6
Association for Career and Technical Education, 4, 37
Augustine, Carl, 74–75, 78–79, 86–88, 90

Barone, Michael, 84–85, 90
Blank, William, 42–43, 55–58, 68–69, 74
Bourdieu, Pierre, 60
Bousquet, Marc, 111–12, 114–16
Boyer, Ernest, 75, 117
Braverman, Harry, 17, 85–86, 89
Bridges, William, 43
Brooks, David, 108–10, 113–14
Bush, George W., 8, 93

California Coalition for Construction in the Classroom, 74
Career Education, 7, 45–48, 50–51, 54, 56–59, 61, 67
Celebrity culture, 14, 84
Choice, as economic ideology, 8, 10, 12, 15, 48–50, 54, 56, 58–59, 61, 98–102, 108, 112
Clark, Burton, 3, 40–41
Class, 4, 10, 22, 46, 57–58, 70, 77, 96–97; division, 14, 22, 36–37, 46, 62, 70, 77; and inequality, 58, 73; processes, 8–10, 14–16, 22–23, 37, 62, 73, 78, 85, 89–91, 92, 94, 98, 100–2, 104–8, 112, 114, 117–18; warfare, 20–21, 31–33, 73, 77. *See also* Exploitation; Hyperindividualism; Middle class; Vocational Education, and class; "Waste" labor; Working class
Clinton, William, 21, 51
College English Association, 95
Competition, intensification of, 1, 11, 14–16, 78–85, 88–92, 94, 98–101, 104, 106, 108, 117
Composition studies, 97, 104, 106, 109–16
Consumer culture, 14, 32–33, 58–59, 61–62, 67, 98
Consumption, and work, 14, 58, 60–62, 65, 71–73, 75, 98–99
Cooling out, 3–4, 8, 40–44, 62, 67–68, 70, 72, 91
Craig, John, 51

123

Cubberley, Ellwood, 46, 58
Cultural capital, 16, 97, 107, 114, 117

Deleuze, Gilles, 22, 36, 66
Dewey, John, 2–3, 18–20, 45–46, 108
Douglass, Frederick, 1–2, 5
Duffy, Elizabeth, 93

Ehrenreich, Barbara, 31
Eng, Lily, 103
English as a discipline, 95–97, 105, 111–14, 117
Entertainment Weekly, 6
Exploitation, 15, 73, 86, 90–91, 97, 99, 104, 114–18. *See also* Class: processes

Financialization, 23–24, 26, 31, 55
Franklin, Benjamin, 1–2, 5

Getting the Job You Really Want, 66
Glassman, Ronald, 23–24, 30–31, 70
Gordon, Howard, 37, 46
Grade inflation, 80–83, 87, 89–90
Grades and grading, 16, 80–83, 87, 89–90, 104, 106, 109
Gray, Kenneth, and Edwin Herr, 26, 39–40, 42, 49, 79, 102
Grubb, W. Norton, 13–14, 40–45, 47, 49, 52–53, 55, 58–59, 69, 71, 79
Guattari, Felix, and Gilles Deleuze, 66

Hardt, Michael, and Antonio Negri, 12–13, 22–23, 28–30, 33, 35–36, 85–86
Harkin, Patricia, 96, 114
Heating up expectations, 3–4, 6–8, 10, 14, 41, 44, 62, 68, 70, 72–73, 79, 82, 91
Heller, Karen, 103
Herr, Edwin, and Kenneth Gray, 26, 39–40, 42, 49, 79, 102

Hibben, John, 109
High Noon, 2, 5–6, 12
Hogg, Cheryl, 45, 48, 55
Home economics, 18, 49
Horowitz, David, 108
Hoyt, Kenneth, 45
Hull, Dan, 49–50, 53–56
Humanities disciplines, 15–16, 61, 95–98, 107–8, 111–14, 116
Hyperindividualism, 14–16, 78, 85, 89–91, 98–101. *See also* Class: processes

Identity, and work, 29–30, 33
Immaterial labor, 12, 28–31, 35–36
Indiana State Teachers Association, 3
Industrial economy, 3, 7, 12, 17–24, 26–27, 32–33, 35–36, 42, 47, 58, 76–77, 90–91, 99
Intelligence testing, 27–28, 34, 36, 69

Job ladder, 53–54
Job mobility, 13–14, 36, 57, 67–68

Keynes, John Maynard, 23
Kimball, Roger, 108
Kniffen, Kevin, 103
Kristol, Irving, 11

Laclau, Ernesto, and Chantal Mouffe, 8–9
Laurence, David, 95–97, 113–14
Lee, Edwin, 18, 37
Leslie, Larry, and Sheila Slaughter, 15, 80, 92, 94–96
Liebow, Elliot, 25, 29
Lifelong education, 7, 13, 19–20, 42
Lipsitz, George, 10
Literacy, 26–27, 95–97, 107, 113, 117
Lopez, Kathryn Jean, 5

Management, 15–16, 32, 46, 93, 108; of academic labor, 15–16, 88–90, 97–98, 102–8, 109–12, 114–17;

Index

corporate, 17, 24, 26, 52–53, 76, 85–86, 88–90, 102–3. *See also* Scientific management
Mann, Horace, 19, 20, 108
Marland, Sidney, Jr., 45
Marx, Karl, 17, 70, 83, 95–96, 99
Marxist analysis, 10, 21, 29, 73, 86, 88, 91
Merit ideologies, 34, 41, 69, 72, 104, 108–9
Middle class, 2–3, 13, 23, 32, 47–48, 50, 57; decline, 11–12, 21–22, 25, 29, 31–32, 38; as emblem of inclusiveness, 10–11, 32–33, 36, 77, 91, 93
Miller, Richard, 109
Modern Language Association, 95
Mouffe, Chantal, and Ernesto Laclau, 8–9

National Alliance of Business, 51
National Center for Educational Statistics, 39
National Center on Education and the Economy, 7
National Education Association (NEA), 102–3
Nealon, Jeffrey, 102–3, 105, 107, 114, 116
Negri, Antonio, and Michael Hardt, 12–13, 22–23, 28–30, 33, 35–36, 85–86
New Literacy studies, 97

Occupational Outlook Handbook, 14, 62–72
Olson, Lynn, 34
O'Neill, Peggy, 115–16

Parnell, Dale, 48–49
Pautler, Albert, 61

Peterson, Wallace, and Frederick Strobel, 20–25, 29–33, 54–55, 58, 73
Phillips, Kevin, 31, 54
Porter, James, 111
Postindustrial economy, 7, 12–13, 21–22, 32–33, 36, 42, 77
Postmodernism, 9
Postsecondary education, 1, 4, 15–16, 41, 43, 48, 94, 96–98, 101, 107, 116, 117, 118. *See also* Undergraduate education; Vocational Education: recent reforms
Proposition 13, in California, 92
Prosser, Charles, 2–3, 7–9, 13, 18–21, 23, 28, 37–38, 46–48, 50, 58–59, 118. *See also* Vocational Education, and class: history of in the United States

Reaganism, 8, 10–12, 21–22, 78
Reich, Robert, 11, 21, 22–26, 28–32, 35, 51
Reserve army of labor, 16, 88–89, 91, 101
Resnick, Lauren, and John Wirt, 19–21, 26, 28, 32–34, 36, 42–43, 58, 65, 99, 108
Resnick, Stephan, and Richard Wolff, 10
Rhoades, Gary, and Sheila Slaughter, 15, 75, 77, 80–81, 92–94, 102–3, 105, 107, 110, 112–13
Rifkin, Jeremy, 99
Robbins, Bruce, 2
Rosenbaum, James, 106

SCANS Guidelines, 7, 13, 43–44, 52–53
School-to-Work Opportunities Act, 34, 51
School-to-Work (STW) program, 13, 51, 57

Scientific management, 17, 86, 89, 90, 105
Searching, for jobs, 14, 61, 64–67, 70–71, 98. *See also* Work, as consumption
Shaping Tomorrow's Workforce, 51
Simulation testing, 28, 33–34, 57, 70
Slaughter, Sheila, 15, 75, 77, 80–81, 92–96, 102–3, 105, 107, 110, 112–13
Smart work, 7, 12–13, 26, 34–35, 37–38, 76–77. *See also* Immaterial labor; Symbolic analysts
Smith-Hughes Act, 2–3, 7, 18, 45
Sneddon, David, 3
Society of control, 22, 36
Strange, Susan, 20–21, 55
Strickland, Donna, 104
Strobel, Frederick, and Wallace Peterson, 20–25, 29–33, 54–55, 58, 73
Student, as consumer, 16, 61, 75
Subsumption, of labor, 85–86, 88–89
Sullivan, Patricia, 111
Super, Donald, 47
Symbolic analysts, 25–26, 28, 30–31, 35

Taylor, Frederick, 17–18, 19–20, 26–27
Tech Prep (TPAD), 13, 48–51, 54–55, 57, 68
Testing, 27–28, 33–34, 36, 57, 62, 69–70, 86, 89, 105–6. *See also* Intelligence testing; Simulation testing
Textual studies, 96–97, 113–15
Thatcherism, 8
Total Quality Management (TQM), 26
Tucker, Marc, 26–28, 33–34, 36, 69

Undergraduate education, 1, 4, 15–16, 75, 81, 87, 92–96, 98, 104, 107, 110. *See also* Postsecondary education; Vocational education: recent reforms
University town, as factory town, 76–77, 91
Upward mobility, 2, 22, 45

Violas, Paul, 46
Vocational education, and class, 2–4, 9–10, 12, 22–23, 32, 45–46, 57–58, 61, 72–73, 90–91, 96–98, 114, 116, 118; history of in the United States, 1–4, 7–8, 12–13, 18–20, 22, 37–38, 45–48; recent reforms, 3–4, 7–10, 12–13, 19–23, 26, 32, 35–37, 42, 45, 48, 55, 58, 61, 68, 70, 74, 83, 93, 99, 108, 114, 116–18. *See also* Postsecondary education; Prosser, Charles; School-to-Work (STW) program; Tech Prep (TPAD); Undergraduate education

"Waste" labor, 15–16, 78, 85, 88–91, 101, 104, 108
Weir, Margaret, 21, 25
Winner-takes-all culture, 37, 39, 45
Wirt, John, and Lauren Resnick, 19–21, 26, 28, 32–34, 36, 42–43, 58, 65, 99, 108
Wolfe, Alan, 11
Wolff, Richard, and Stephan Resnick, 10
Work, as consumption, 14, 58, 60–62, 65, 71–73, 75, 98–99. *See also* Searching, for jobs
Working class, 3–4, 9, 22, 46–47, 50, 58, 90–91
Writing Across the Curriculum, 111